VALUE DEVELOPMENT

...AS THE AIM OF EDUCATION

WITHDRAWN

edited by:

Norman A. Sprinthall

and

Ralph L. Mosher

WITHDRAWN

Character Research Press
207 State Street
Schenectady, New York 12305 U.S.A.

International Standard Book Number 0-915744-10-4
Library of Congress Catalog Card No. L.C. 78-68113
First Printing

WITHDRAWN

TABLE OF CONTENTS

Page

A Primer on Development

Norman A. Sprinthall

In order to acquaint the reader with some of the basic assumptions (and equally basic theoretical contributions) upon which programs of developmental education have been constructed, we will present a brief review of developmental constructs. Most of the theorists to be described in this primer are referred to at both the conceptual and operational level in the articles that follow. Thus, a review was felt to be a help.

Moreover, it will be obvious (from the articles that follow) that our view is that no single developmental theory is an adequate overall framework within which to comprehend human growth. At the moment, then, we are content to conceptualize growth from a series of discreet, yet related, perspectives. The general advantage of such multiple perspectives in this area is obvious, and has been well stated by Peatling in a recent issue of Character Potential.[1] We need only add that it is our assessment of the current state of theory and practice for developmental education that we are required to continue to look for concordance and confirmatory evidence across a series of theories. At the operational level, especially, we have argued for the need of multiple measures.

For example, by not placing all of our eggs in one measurement basket, so to speak, we can be on less tenuous ground when empirical findings are consistent across a series of developmental domains. This advantage at the empirical level is also matched by advantage at the conceptual level. A single human being is and always will be more complex than any single theory (or, even, a grand and possibly synergistic grouping of multiple theories) would lead one to believe. However, we feel that it is possible to at least gain on the problem (and the paradox) of human understanding by employing a variety of developmental perspectives.

At the present time, the chief theorists around whom we work are Dewey, Piaget, Kohlberg, Loevinger, and Selman. Although we don't use all of them all of the time, the reader will find a general overlap of theorists throughout the articles that follow this introductory primer. However, we want to begin by briefly outlining a key developmental assumption: that is, development proceeds through a sequence of qualitatively different stages, invariantly, so that each stage builds on the previous stage in an hierarchical manner.

Developmental Stages:
From Egg to Caterpillar to Butterfly

The concept of a "stage of development" is central to the thought and work of each of the four theorists we will consider in this review. It was, of course, John Dewey who originally formed the idea that children and teenagers move through stages of development.[2] In this view, a child is not a midget-sized adult who simply "grows" from small to large in some quantitative sense. Instead, children and teenagers grow and develop in a series of qualitatively distinct stages. Each such stage is unique; it is a special way of organizing the thought process and, so, involves a special way for a person to make meaning or understand the world. Such qualitative growth can be compared to the transformations involved in the sequence from an egg to a caterpillar to a butterfly. Each stage of development is, then, unique and separate, yet each succeeding stage builds upon and is (in fact) dependent upon the prior stage. Moreover, the "direction" of such a developmental sequence is both invariant and irreversible.

For example: it is to be expected that, as a pupil develops,

Norman A. Sprinthall

there will be a major shift in terms of that pupil's general cognitive process, and that such a shift (or, better, shifts) will occur at specific age-related points. Whether or not growth and development occurs (i.e., there is a movement from a stage to its next sequential stage) depends, however, upon the kind and the quality of the person's interaction with the environment. This is a crucial point: indeed, it may well be the most important aspect of developmental theory and practice. Growth does not take place automatically. Development as a sequential process is not a unilateral unfolding. Instead, a person needs a series of significant experiences (i.e., interactions with the environment) at particular times, for it is such experiences that promote the shift from a lower stage to a next higher stage of development. Without such significant experiences at certain critical times, a person will cease psychological growth and, prematurely, stabilize at some stage that is below his or her developmental potential.

From such a developmental perspective, adolescence can be regarded as a stage in which almost all persons can learn to function at relatively high levels in any of the theoretical sequences of cognitive, moral, ego or interpersonal growth. However, whether an individual learns to so function (i.e., to grow to a particular level) depends upon the general educational experience of that individual. At other developmental stages, particular learnings may be requisite for an individual's continued comprehensive growth which, in turn, may be a necessary lead into a stage.

Cognitive Development:
The Theory of Jean Piaget

Jean Piaget has been a most important source of psychological knowledge concerning general cognitive growth and development.[3] His contribution has been fundamental: he has detailed the stage sequence of stages of cognitions, especially during childhood and adolescence. His general theory of periods and stages is outlined in *Table I.*

Value Development 3

Table I
PIAGET'S STAGES OF COGNITIVE DEVELOPMENT

Stage I   (Birth to 2 years)   SENSORI-MOTOR Stage

During this Stage, learning is based primarily on immediate experience through the five senses. The child has perceptions and movements as his only tools for learning. Lacking language, the child does not yet have the ability to represent or symbolize thinking and, thus, has no way to categorize experiences. One of the first sensori-motor abilities to develop is that of visual pursuit (i.e., the ability to perceive and hold a visual object with the eyes). Later, the child develops the capacity of object permanence (i.e., the ability to understand that an object can still exist, even though it cannot be seen). Lacking vision during this period prevents the growth of mental structures.

**Stage II   (2 to 7 years)   PRE-OPERATIONAL
                                     or INTUITIVE Stage**

During this Stage the child is no longer bound to the immediate sensory environment, and it builds upon abilities (such as object permanence) from the sensori-motor stage. The ability to store mental images and symbols (e.g., words, and language as a structure for words) increases dramatically. The mode of learning is a freely-experimenting, intuitive one that is, quite generally, unconcerned with reality. Communication occurs in collective monologues, in which children talk to themselves more than they do to each other. Use of language during this Stage is, therefore, both ego-centric and spontaneous. Although use of language is the major learning focus at this Stage, many other environmental discoveries are made by the child, who uses a generally freewheeling, intuitive approach to the environment.

**Stage III   (7 to 12 years)   CONCRETE
                                       OPERATIONAL Stage**

During this Stage there is a dramatic shift in the child's learning strategy from intuition to concrete thought. Reality-bound thinking takes over, and the child must test out problems in order to understand them. The difference between dreams and facts can be clearly distinguished, but that between an hypothesis and a fact cannot. The child becomes overly logical and concrete, so that once its mind is made up new facts will not change it. Facts and order become absolutes during this Stage.

**Stage IV   (12 years and older)   FORMAL
                                          OPERATIONAL Stage**

At this Stage the child enters adolescence, and the potential for developing full, formal patterns of thinking emerges. The adolescent is capable of attaining logical-rational (or abstract) strategies. Symbolic meanings, metaphors, and similes can now be understood. Implications can be drawn, and generalizations can be made.

4   **Norman A. Sprinthall**

Piaget has suggested that it is *only* during adolescence (i.e., *not before* adolescence) that an individual is capable of certain modes of thought. What he has called "formal operations" in thought provide an individual the opportunity to think in ways that are qualitatively different from the ways of thinking possible during childhood. For instance, an adolescent *can* conceive of possibilities and probabilities. An adolescent can think abstractly about himself. An adolescent's sense of time perspective changes and, so, he can perceive himself in a variety of ways, both now and in the future. Such a new mode of perceiving and of understanding oneself is tremendously significant, if we are at all concerned about so-called personal questions. *If* an adolescent pupil is capable of:

(a) *Thinking about himself in a non-absolutist way,* rather than tending as children do to categorize along such dimensions as good/bad, or white hats/black hats; and is also capable of. . .

(b) *Conceiving of self and future in terms of probability trends and possibilities,* rather than tending as children do to see their futures already determined; and is also capable of. . .

(c) *Changing his hypotheses as new information is brought to light,* rather than tending as children do to "hang on" to hypotheses, in spite of new and contradictory evidence;

then an educator has an opportunity for deliberate education.

One of the major shortcomings of schooling, particularly of the so-called standard curriculum of secondary schools, has been a *failure* to *promote* the use of Piaget's "formal operations" of thought. Estimates vary, but all indicate that only between 25% and 50% of the secondary school pupils actually develop an ability to use formal operations in their thinking. While *almost all* such students are potentially *able* to learn to use formal operations in their thinking, a substantial number do *not* ever *achieve* a level of thinking that uses "formal operations."[4] From both a theoretical and a quite practical perspective, this failure *limits* future growth and development during post-adolescence (i.e., adulthood).

Moral Development:
The Theory of Lawrence Kohlberg

In the area of moral development, the recent work of Lawrence Kohlberg is particularly significant.[5] Based on a long series of field interviews, which were designed to find out how humans actually think about problems of social justice, Kohlberg discovered that the process of making judgments actually formed a developmental sequence of six stages. After investigating the judgments of people of different ages, different social classes and different economic classes, as well as the judgments of people in different cultures, Kohlberg found a sequence of stage growth parallel to that Piaget had found. Essentially following Piaget's method of the clinical interview, Kohlberg interviewed persons using an open-ended format. His questions were focused upon matters of social justice, fairness, and ethics, rather than upon the questions of time, space, or causality that Piaget had already investigated. Kohlberg asked people essentially one question: What *should* a person do when confronted with a human dilemma (e.g., the "necessity" to steal, in order to save another human life)?

Based upon his findings, Kohlberg's view is that *all* humans *do* think about such questions of social justice. Moreover, the ways people do think about such questions represent a series of distinct and qualitatively different stages of moral judgment. Thus, we are all "moral philosophers," although we use different systems of thought to reach our several conclusions. Both Kohlberg and Piaget speak of, "the child and the adolescent as moral philosophers." This phrase means that humans do ponder questions such as the meaning of

Norman A. Sprinthall

human existence, the meaning of rightness and wrongness (and their difference), and the conditions under which one will help another human being. The form (or "structure") of one's thinking about such questions, as well as the judgments one reaches as a result of that thinking, is distinctly different in the several stages of development. By examining the "structure" of thinking and judging which his interviewees employed, Kohlberg was able to group their "styles" of thinking and judging into three basic levels and six sequential stages. These levels and stages are outlined in *Table II*.

Research has shown that, from a developmental standpoint, a person's level of moral-judgment thinking tends to lag slightly behind his/her general stage of cognitive development. Thus, although almost 50% of the adolescents in the United States do reach some level of formal, abstract thought, only between 25% and 30% of those adolescents reach Kohlberg's Stage 5 in their moral judgment thinking.[6] This result is understandable, once we realize that problems of social justice are (a) more complex, (b) more subjective, and (c) more personally involving, than are the problems of general abstract level thinking. Moreover, as it is quite obvious in these times of a post-Watergate morality, educational experience (even or especially at the secondary school level) in responding to general moral questions is usually very limited.

Schooling has tended to avoid direct interaction with questions of social justice, or with problems of values. Society at large has also eschewed just such questions. Usually this strategy of ignorance has been disguised by either a narrow-minded literal moralism or, perhaps just as often, by an atheoretical pragmatism. However, whatever the reason, Kohlberg has found that the majority of teenagers "stabilize" their moral judgment thinking somewhere between his Stage 3 and his Stage 4. This means that *most* high school pupils employ a system of moral judgment thought which *assumes* that "justice" means either (a) going along with the crowd (i.e., the other-directedness of Stage 3), or (b) rigidly applying a stan-

Table II

KOHLBERG'S STAGES OF MORAL DEVELOPMENT

Level I   The PRE-CONVENTIONAL Level

At this Level, moral value resides in external, quasi-physical happenings (e.g., bad acts) or in quasi-physical needs (e.g., food to eat), rather than in either persons or standards.

> **Stage I**   Obedience and punishment orientation.
>
> > Egocentric deference to superior power or prestige, or a trouble-avoiding set. Objective responsibility.
>
> **Stage 2**   Naively egoistic orientation.
>
> > Right action is that which is instrumentally satisfying of the self's needs and, only occasionally, satisfying of others' needs. Awareness of a relativism of value to each actor's needs and perspectives. Naive egalitarianism, and an orientation to exchange and reciprocity.

Level II   The CONVENTIONAL Level

At this Level, moral value resides in performing good or right roles, in maintaining the conventional order, and in meeting the expectancies of others.

> **Stage 3**   Good-boy orientation.
>
> > An orientation to approval, and to pleasing and helping others. Conformity to stereotypical images of the majority (or natural) role behavior, and judgment in terms of intentions.
>
> **Stage 4**   Authority-and-Social-Order-maintaining orientation.
>
> > An orientation to doing one's duty, and to showing respect for authority, and to maintaining the given social order for its own sake. Regard for the earned expectations of others.

Level III   The POST-CONVENTIONAL Level

At this Level, moral value resides in conformity by the self to shared (or sharable) standards, rights, or duties.

> **Stage 5**   Contractual legalistic orientation.
>
> > There is a recognition of an arbitrary element or starting point in either rules or expectations, for the sake of agreement. Duty is defined in terms of a contract, a general avoidance of a violation of the will or the rights of others, and the majority will and welfare.
>
> **Stage 6**   Conscience or principle orientation.
>
> > An orientation not only to actually ordained social rules but to those principles of choice which involve an appeal to logical universality and consistnecy. An orientation to conscience as a directing agent, and to mutual respect and trust.

           Norman A. Sprinthall

dard of law-and-order, regardless of the circumstances (i.e., the social-order-maintaining orientation of Stage 4). Without new significant interactions with their environment, most teenagers enter adulthood with rather stereotyped systems of thinking about, and making judgments about the major questions of legal- and moral-justice. Unfortunately, as our society and our educational practice is currently organized, the person's system of thinking tends to undergo few changes after adolescence. As we noted in the previous section on Piaget's theory of cognitive development, growth to the place where one uses "formal operations" and, so, engages in abstract thinking, demands a stimulating curriculum (i.e., the curriculum needs to actually promote, not just assume, development). It would seem that the same need exists if adolescents are to develop their ability to think about and make moral judgments about the ever-present questions of social justice.

Ego Development:
The Theory of Jane Loevinger

Based upon an extensive series of field interviews, Jane Loevinger has created a framework that helps one comprehend the stages in the development of the ego.[7] She sees the ego as a master trait of personal growth, much in the manner of other theorists, such as Gordon Allport and Robert White. Therefore, ego is a construct which refers to that part of human personality that acts as an executive: that is, ego is involved in coordinating, choosing, selecting and directing a person's activities.

Loevinger's work suggests that there are special qualities of ego functioning (e.g., how adequately or inadequately a person chooses, or makes decisions). At different stages of development, Loevinger suggests that the ego functions in distinctly different ways or patterns. At the higher stages of development, the ego functions more adequately (i.e., takes in more aspects of a given situation, views problems with a greater tolerance for complexity, sees things more broadly, and selects from a greater variety of possible actions). As the outline in *Table III* indicates, there are clear qualitative differences to the various stages of ego development that Loevinger has discerned. Each one of her stages builds upon the previous stage, but it exhibits a higher level of differentiation and integration. Thus, these Loevinger stages can be viewed as a sequence of developmental stages leading toward personal growth and development.

Table III
LOEVINGER'S "MILESTONES" OF EGO DEVELOPMENT

Stage:	Code:	IMPULSE CONTROL, and/or CHARACTER DEVELOPMENT:
Presocial	I - 1	
Symbiotic		
Impulsive	I - 2	Impulsive, fear of retaliation.
Self-Protective	△	Fear of being caught, externalizing blame, opportunistic.
Conformist	I - 3	Conformity to external rules, shame, guilt for breaking rules.
Conscientious	I - 4	Self-evaluated standards, self-criticism, guilt for consequences, long-term goals and ideals.
Autonomous	I - 5	(In addition to Level I - 4, *add*) Coping with conflicting inner needs, toleration.
Integrated	I - 6	(In addition to Level I - 5, *add*) Reconciling inner conflicts, renunciation of unattainable.

NOTE: Table III is based upon a table entitled, "Some Milestones of Ego Development," by Jane Loevinger and Ruth Wessler, which they published in the following book:

Loevinger, Jane, and Ruth Wessler. *Measuring Ego Development, Vol. 1.* (San Francisco: Jossey-Bass, Publ., 1970.)

Norman A. Sprinthall

Studies based upon an extrapolation from Loevinger's ego stages indicate that pupils in elementary school tend to cluster at her ego Stages I - 1, I - 2, and I - 3, while teenagers and young adults tend to range from her delta (Δ) Stage through her I - 4 Stage, with either Stage I - 3 or an intermediate stage between Stages I - 3 and I - 4 as the mode. These results mean that an elementary school pupil tends to have a system of understanding, both the "self" and others, which is concrete and somewhat stereotyped. Adolescents tend to have a system that is more abstract than the elementary school pupils, yet is still highly conformist. There is, of course, an obvious similarity to the stages of moral development outlined in *Table II.*

Kohlberg's Stage 3 appears to be similar to Loevinger's Stage I - 3 and the intermediate stage between Stage I - 3 and Stage I - 4. This similarity seems to mean that the major preoccupations of the teenage ego are with concepts such as (a) conformity for its own sake, or (b) superficial niceness, or (c) the importance of appearance, or (d) social acceptability, or even (e) stereotypical thinking. In addition, the results of the Loevinger-based studies tend to provide cross-validation for the earlier, classic research on adolescence by James Coleman.[8] However, Loevinger's theory provides a broader conceptual framework than Coleman's research, since she charts the nature and structure of still higher stages of ego development.

In both Loevinger's test samples and in some of our own studies, adults tend to stabilize at a slightly higher ego stage level than teenagers. However, this level of stability is at either the intermediate stage between Stage I - 3 and Stage I - 4 or at Stage I - 4 itself. In any of the studies of adults conducted to this time, there are very few adults who consistently function at a level of ego development higher than Stage I - 4 (i.e., very few adults appear to be functioning at Loevinger's Stage I - 5 or her Stage I - 6). What Loevinger has called Stage I - 3 (i.e., Conformist) is highly stable and modal for teenagers. What she has identified as an intermediate stage between Stage I - 3 and Stage I - 4 (i.e., Conscientious) appears to be similarly stable and modal for adults in general.

Interpersonal Development:
The Work of Selman and DuPont

In addition to the work and theoretical contributions of Piaget, Kohlberg and Loevinger on the development and growth of cognition, moral judgment and the ego, the most recent work of Robert Selman requires mention. This work is so new that it can barely be considered as a theory *per se.* Yet, it is clearly both promising and directing.[9] Essentially Selman has "opened up" the whole interpersonal domain to a developmental perspective. That in itself is a considerable accomplishment; one for which we can only be glad that it has happened.

Selman's logic seems to be clear, almost classically so. For example, he poses the fundamental question in the following way. *If* humans can be said to process in stage and sequence their questions of (a) time, space and causality, and of (b) ethical and social justice, and of (c) the self and the ego-domains, *then* can it be doubted that humans also process their questions about interpersonal relationships in terms of developmental stages and sequences? As of this writing, Selman has begun to document social perspective taking within a generally developmental format. His exploratory studies indicate that elementary school pupils and secondary school students understand interpersonal relationships (i.e., engage in social perspective taking) according to the stage sequence that is outlined in *Table IV.*

Selman's five-stage sequence seems to mean that how an individual understands the nature of the interpersonal world (in the Harry Stack Sullivan sense of that phrase) will be governed by the qualitative stage system used. As a result, it is clear that the wildly intuitive interpersonal world of the child between 3 years and 7 years of age (e.g., a world complete with magical friends, and animals that talk) is qualita-

Norman A. Sprinthall

Table IV

SELMAN'S
STAGES OF INTERPERSONAL DEVELOPMENT

STAGES:		DESCRIPTION OF STAGE: Interpersonal Relations and Kinds of Social Role-Taking	AGE RANGE in C.A.:
Codes:	Stage Titles:		
0	Ego Centric	Parallel play--difficulty in distinguishing between self and others.	03 - 06
1	Social-Informational	Can see own perspective and one other person's, yet the main focus remains on self.	06 - 08
2	Self-Reflective	Sequential role-taking. Can understand self and other's perspective in concrete terms, but not simultaneously (e.g., "taking turns")	08 - 10
3	Mutual	Beginning of mutual role-taking, simultaneous process of self and others, but still largely concrete framework.	10 - 12
4	Social and Conventional Role-Taking	Awareness of subjective nature of interpersonal relations. Greater depth of feelings. Abstract and simultaneous perceptions. e.g., "The adolescent as a psychologist."	12 - 15

tively different from that concrete interpersonal world of the child between 7 years and 10 years of age (e.g., a world in which one can "take turns," and understand that persons can experience emotions, one at a time). Much the same thing - - qualitative difference - - appears to be true of the shift during adolescence from sequential role-taking to simultaneous role-taking. Moreover, it is clear that it is this shift that creates the possibilities of multiple perspective-taking, genuine empathy, and the simultaneous processing of multiple emotions in self and others.

In this area of the development of interpersonal relations we should also mention the very recent work of DuPont.[10] DuPont is explicitly documenting the qualitative stages involved in the processing of emotions. When complete, this work should help to fill out the knowledge base in the interpersonal/emotional domain of human development.

Concluding Comments

This primer on development has been written for only one reason: so that the reader may become acquainted with those developmental perspectives that we and our colleagues employ. These perspectives are used by us as both directing constructs and as a way of making an empirical assessment of the outcome of our efforts. They remind us and, hopefully, they will also remind the reader that "development" does not occur unilaterally, nor does it unfold magically. The theories that we have reviewed here function, for us, in both a descriptive and, at least partially, prescriptive manner.

It seems simple. If we know what development *is*, then, with Dewey and others, we know something of what education *ought* to be. The reader will find in the following articles abundant examples of our *oughts*. That is, the reader will find in these articles plentiful evidence of our attempts to stimulate and nurture the process of human growth. This review of the sequence of stages posited by Piaget, Kohlberg, Loevinger and Selman should make what we have been about clear and understandable. At least that is our intention.

REFERENCES

1. Peatling, J. H. "The Advantage of Multiple Perspectives," in *Character Potential: A Record of Research* (Vol. 8, No. 2, August, 1977), pp. 55-56.

2. Dewey, J. *Experience and Education.* (New York: Collier, 1963).

3. Piaget, J. *Science of Education and the Psychology of the Child.* (New York: Viking, 1970).

4. Kohlberg, L., and C. Gilligan. "The Adolescent as Philosopher," in *Daedalus* (100, 1971), pp. 1051-1086.

5. Kohlberg, L. "Stage and Sequence: The Cognitive-Developmental Approach to Socialization," in D. Goslin (Ed.) *The Handbook of Socialization Theory.* (Chicago: Rand McNally, 1969), pp.347-480.

6. Kohlberg, L., and C. Gilligan, *Op. Cit.,* 1971.

7. Loevinger, J. *Ego Development.* (San Francisco: Jossey-Bass, 1976).

8. Coleman, J. *The Adolescent Society.* (New York: Free Press, 1961).

9. Selman, R. "A Developmental Approach to Interpersonal and Moral Awareness in Young Children," in T. Hennessey (Ed.) *Values and Moral Development.* (New York: Paulist Press, 1976), pp. 142-166.

10. DuPont, H. *Toward Affective Development.* (Circle Pines, Minn.: American Guidance Services, 1974).

John Dewey Revisited:
A Framework for
Developmental Education

Norman A. Sprinthall
Ralph L. Mosher

In the last decade we have witnessed the gradual erosion of confidence within the educational establishment to confront and indeed solve the multiple problems of schooling. The optimism of the early 60's was fueled with monies from the "new frontier" and the "great society," with the promise of new educational ideology, and manned by a new cadre of energetic personnel. It seemed that we were on the brink of a major advance. New schooling would promote educational equality on one hand, and the disappearance of the barriers of class and caste on the other. Some few years later, with the advantage of perspective, it now seems so easy, almost facile, to realize that the optimism was misplaced.

The problems of schooling were simply too complex for the brainstormed short-term solution. Behavior modification was only a quick and ineffective technological "fix." The human potential movement with free and open schools, store fronts and otherwise, was romantic but still a brief encounter. The curriculum reformers similarly pushed their own singular theme. Change the content and change the schools, they asserted. This produced massive amounts of new nationally approved material (the new physics, the new social studies, the new math, et. al.). Yet, as Flanagan's massive study has shown, what the pupils really learned from these materials remained disappointingly little.[1] Schooling in practice was affected almost not at all. A few cosmetic changes were made but none successfully grappled with the generic problems.

The roots were unaffected.

In a somewhat simplified sense, the proposals and projects of the 60's attempted to solve only part of the educational problem. With the benefit of hindsight, the prevailing theories at the time were too narrow in focus, providing single variable solutions to multivariate problems. And, if we are honest in reviewing our own careers, we were part of the problem rather than the solution. In fact, some of our writings in the mid-60's clearly reveal that we were riding our own singular hobby horses with just as much fervor as other proponents were theirs.[2] At the same time, we were willing, in the face of negative findings, to shift our focus (gradually) to a broader theory and practice for education.

Even more important, we began in 1968 to commit ourselves to a lengthy series of field investigators, short-cycle tryouts, and careful evaluations of promising and emergent programs. It was during this period when we discarded some of the more traditional theories of curriculum development and psychology applied to school practice. To make a long story brief, this was the time of discovering and re-discovering Dewey in his original form and of Piaget, Kohlberg, Selman, Hunt, Loevinger and William Perry, the more **contemporaneous** exemplars. Through the careful observation of adolescents in secondary schools, we became convinced that a developmental approach to education might represent theory and practice that was both complex enough to comprehend the problems of schooling and operational enough to provide for trial solutions.[3] Then we set off on our own steep and thorny path (a different version of **Pilgrim's Progress**) to build new curriculum approaches and new teaching strategies designed to promote the whole development of the pupil. Some examples are described in detail in the articles that follow. Yet, before we turn to the specifics, it seems appropriate to re-examine some of the constructs and issues central to the developmental perspective.

Value Development 17

A Developmental Perspective:
John Dewey[4]

Archambault, in his preface to **John Dewey on Education**, has said, "It is commonplace that everyone talks about Dewey and no one reads him."[5] A careful reading, even now, will reveal that his argument that "the aim of education is development of individuals to the utmost of their potentialities" is still the clearest philosophical rationale for the education we are creating. In a succinct essay that Dewey published originally in 1934, "The Need for a Philosophy of Education," Dewey makes a series of telling points: "What then is education when we find actual satisfactory specimens of it in existence? In the first place, it is a process of development of growth and it is the process, and not merely the result, that is important . . . an educated person is the person who has the power to go on and get more education."[6]

Dewey then makes the point that Rousseau's notion of *natural* development (i.e., human beings, analogous to seeds, have latent capacities which, if only they are left to themselves, will ultimately flower and bear fruit), has at least two fallacies. The *first* is that people are vastly more complex in their development and potential than plants, the *second* is that development is a matter of the *kind of interaction* that occurs between the organism and its environment. Nature and nurture, in interaction, produce development. Dewey argued that development (or education) starts with the pupil. "Every mind, even of the youngest, is naturally or inherently seeking for those modes of active operation that are within the limits of its capacity . . . The problem, a difficult and delicate one, is to discover what tendencies are especially seeking expression at a particular time and just what materials and methods will serve to evoke and direct a truly educative development."[7] What Dewey didn't and couldn't know was what indeed characterizes development, whether it be intellectual, moral or social, at a particular stage or time in the person's life.

Sprinthall and Mosher

A generation of research in genetic epistemology and developmental psychology by such people as Piaget, Kohlberg, Loevinger, and others, *now* offers educators relatively clear blueprints of what people are like at various stages in their lives and what it is that stimulates their intellectual, moral and personal-social growth. This information, available to us and not to Dewey, says much, in developmental "fact," about that remarkably prophetic phrase, "the tendencies especially seeking expression at a particular time." What developmental psychology does not concern itself with, but developmental *education* does, is "just what materials and methods will serve to evoke and direct a truly educative development." But of that, which is the genuinely original thing we are learning or contributing, more later.

There is little need here to examine Dewey's critique of traditional education - - the external and authoritative imposition of subject matter and skills which he compared quaintly to "inscribing records upon a passive phonographic disc to result in giving back what has been inscribed when the proper button is pressed in recitation or examination." That system (and its more contemporary critique) is still too much with us, as we have noted, for further comment. Criticism in the final analysis is cheap; constructive reformulation of educational practice is much harder work. But our critique of the schools adolescents attend, in the original **American Psychologist** article, is absolutely fundamental to understanding our continuing odyssey in developmental education.[8]

Dewey's more important point to progressive education was *not* to stop short with the recognition of the importance of giving free scope to native capacities and interests. This is really another statement of the "don't fall into the Rousseau trap or all you have to do is get out of the child's way." One has the impression that much of the criticism of progressivism as a "country-club existentialism" or "directionless activity" may have resulted from progressive educators and critics who genuinely misunderstood how much more than that Dewey was saying: both about the intricate characteristics of development in children and how they have to be seen as potentialities/processes, which are not enduring or end points but which, with experience and time, will themselves evolve profoundly.

The special obligation of the educator to profoundly understand the psychology of cognitive, moral and social development is part of the charge which Dewey was anticipating. The other part has to do with the core task of developmental education. That is the devising, and the testing of the curricula (i.e., those systematic educational experiences which permit the person continually to grow from experience). Dewey anticipated something we are learning - - that we have to pay more, not less, attention to the subject matter and pedagogy of developmental education. Devising and validating those experiences that, indeed, affect development is far more complex than rewriting curriculum in American history or literature. There are just far more knowns, precedents and criteria for doing the latter.

"The great problems of the adult who has to deal with the young is to see, and to feel deeply as well as merely to see intellectually, the forces that are moving in the young; but it is to see them as possibilities, as signs and promises; to interpret them, in short, in the light of what they may come to be. Nor does the task end there. It is bound up with the further problem of judging and devising the conditions, the materials, both physical, such as tools of work, and moral and social, which will, once more, so *interact* with existing powers and preferences as to bring about transformation in the desired direction."[9]

The point is that it would be nearly a generation before the first part of this metaphor, i.e., "to see intellectually the forces that are moving in the young," would be translated into comprehensive empirical psychological data or knowledge. We will detail more about that knowledge of development in the next section. Moreover, it is really only in the past five years that the educational work of translating the second part of the metaphor "devising the conditions . . . which will . . . so interact with existing powers . . . to bring about transformation," into concrete curriculum with developmental effects has begun. Again, how rigorously that must be done was anticipated by Dewey. "If we do not go on and go far in the positve direction of providing a body of subject matter much richer, more varied and flexible, and also in truth more definite . . . than traditional education supplied, we shall tend to leave an educational vacuum in which anything can happen."[10] A valid supposition is that this is what the progressive educators couldn't bring off. Why is a complex story, part of which Lawrence Cremin tells in **The Transformation of the American School.**[11]

In our view, some of that why had to do with the fact that the psychological knowledge of the stages, characteristics and experiences contributing to human development available to the progressive educators was grossly inadequate. In any event, the project method is a pretty light-weight translation of what Dewey was calling for. Maybe current or subsequent critics of developmental education will similarly damn our efforts with faint praise. The charge remains, however - - as does the consequence of ineptitude. "The young live in some environment whether we intend it or not and this environment is constantly interacting with what children bring to it, and the result is the shaping of their interests - - minds and character - - either educatively or miseducatively. If the professed educator abdicates his responsibility for judging and selecting the kind of environment that his best understanding leads him to think will be conducive to growth, then the young are left at the mercy of all the unorganized and casual forces of the modern social environment that inevitably play upon them as long as they live."[12]

From our view today, there is one important philosophical flaw in this conception of development as the aim of education. It is with Dewey's original conception of humankind. As Professor Beck has noted, Dewey dwelt too little on interpersonal relations.[13] Thus, a man or woman for Dewey was part of a faceless collective, a group, or a general social problem. Individual development, especially in the realm of how each person interacts, was a major gap in his educational theory. Fortunately, some of the more recent developmental work, particularly of Kohlberg on individual ethical interactions, Selman's interpersonal, Hunt and Perry's epistomological transactions, and Loevinger's ego levels, all provide a more focused view on how each individual interrelates with the environmental press. Or, to update Dewey's dictum, how *each* organism interacts with its own environment.

Dewey makes two additional points in his essay which have profound meaning for contemporary developmental education. He says development is a continuous process, and that means the experiences or action which stimulate development will have a quality of consecutiveness - - of planned order. He warned that "it is comparatively easy to improvise, to try a little of this today and this week and then something else tomorrow and next week . . . without care and thought (this) results all too readily, in a detached multiplicity of isolated short-time activities or projects and the continuity necessary for growth is lost."[14]

An honest appraisal of the curriculum we outlined in the 1970 **American Psychologist** article would see it as vulnerable to this charge; our present curricula as discussed in the following section are relatively much less so. But we are still some distance from the curricula or the knowledge by which to order experiences to stimulate consecutive development. We perceive the need and the outline of how to get there, but much development and testing remains to be done. This is the essential raison d'etre of developmental education.

Essentially, then, what this book contains is some of the most recent examples of translating the overall objective of development as the aim of education into practice. Some of these studies are as highly specific as a one term course for adolescents or middle schoolers or elementary pupils. Others are broader, such as teachers or parents as developmental educators. Finally, there is a discussion of some of the most recent and broad-gauge attempts to re-structure a model "school within a school" to an entire school system. These are not isolated examples. There are a series of earlier so-called first generation studies in this developmental genre published elsewhere which are consistent and complementary to the present studies.[15] This book, then, provides additional examples which confirm previous findings and break new ground. The overall problem of school reform, as we noted at the outset, is immensely complex. We have moved, at least somewhat systematically, from the problems of how to design individual classroom environments to the larger questions of new modes for teacher education and the organization of schools as systems. The developmental dictum of interaction (or person-environment match) forces the educator to consider the implications across the board.

At the same time, and as a final point, we do wish to underscore our present understanding of the concept of development.

Human Development and Perfectibility?

In the 18th Century during the Age of Enlightenment, Condorcet and other philosophers somewhat naively suggested that human beings could become perfect. The conception of human development was broad. Through our developing rational faculties we could master the world in all forms, including the physical and spiritual. The perfectibility of mankind was pronounced. The conception was dazzling. The "Age of Reason" would lead to a heaven on earth. The sun would shine within our lifetimes. Camelot was possible. The development of rationalism would forever banish the Dark Ages. All the difficulties of human development, of interdependence, of freedom, were no longer unsolvable. Nature never made a dunce, as Helvetius would say. The problems of human growth became opportunities for rational problem solving. Such a bold, imaginative and breath-taking conception could simply sweep away all opposition. Only the weak-willed could resist such a vision. Progress and reason had become the new ideology.

We now realize, of course, that the narrow pre-Freudian rationalism with its ideas of human perfectibility and the unlimited human potential for growth, were based on assumptions which fell spectacularly short of actualization. In fact, most of the 20th Century stands as a horrifying object lesson. Instead of rationalism triumphant, it has seemed as if irrationalism reigned. In place of perfection, grotesque imperfection. Rather than a heaven on earth, a hell. Instead of positive learning from experience, the 20th Century has almost seemed like a nightmare, replicated in ever worsening magnitude. The scale of atrocities has increased through demonic quantum leaps. From twenty million dead in World War I, we escalated to fifty-five million dead in World War II. From bombs that could devastate a city block, we progressed to those that could demolish an entire city . . . .

In face of this, what can be said of development? Can we still seriously consider the possibility of development as a significant human goal? Wouldn't it seem more logical to accept the lessons of the 20th Century as a massive assault on such democratic assumptions? Doesn't logic compel us to assume that civilization is at best an extremely thin veneer and, at worst, an illusion? Man to man is, in this view, an errant wolf. Civilization's only hope is, then, a policy of containment. Certainly there are times when, in summing up this Century, it would be difficult to add up to development.

We have tried to make the point in this issue that development, in spite of all the obvious shortcomings, seems like the most promising idea we have. It's almost like Churchill's famous phrase about democracy as a form of government - - completely inadequate yet better than all others. We do, however, make one qualification. We do hope that our conception of human development has been tempered through the experience of the first half of the 20th Century. Otherwise, it will surely seem as if the only progress we've made is toward degeneracy.

On the other hand, the emerging conception of human development in moral as well as psychological terms provides a basis for informed choice by educators. By definition, our role is a complex one. We are not social scientists commenting from the side-lines. We are convinced that theory and practice are not separate and, in fact, have reversed the usual dictum. For us it is theory from practice. Thus, in this sense, we back into theory as a means of explaining and comprehending the effects of our practice. The role of a moral/developmental educator, in our view, is to work in educational settings, not laboratories, and through practice to improve the developmental functioning of children, teenagers, and teachers.

We hope that the objective of stimulating natural development is not simply begging the means-ends question, nor, merely a *tours-de-force.* Finally, we hope it is not a neo-vision of human perfectibility. We are interested, along with Friere[16] and others, in enhancing the practice of freedom. Yet, we also know full well that not all the answers are in. It is not time to close the patent office for a section entitled Developmental Education. Not only do we need a focused effort on particular programs to increase moral and psychological development and behavior, which (by definition) will be different at different stages, we also can't assume that teachers will be automatically capable to implement developmental/moral education.

We have a long way to go and we know it. In fact, one of the most helpful remarks that Kohlberg made to us when we started in the late 60's was to caution us to go slowly. Don't leap into polished curriculum guides. Avoid the temptation to go "public" with the advent of the initial promising findings.

In sum, we are at a critical junction, indeed almost a transition stage, for developmental education. Without belaboring the point, the schools of the country are not meeting the needs of pupils. The work in developmental education is a promising beginning. Experience and reflection in a guided sequence can yield a fruitful harvest for democracy. Citizens of the future can be helped to understand and, so, to act upon the significant questions involved in the practice of freedom. The critical need now is for careful, yet gradual, expansion.

NOTES and REFERENCES

1. Flanagan, J., "Education: How and for What" in *American Psychologist* (28, 1973), pp. 551-556.

2. See N. A. Sprinthall, *Guidance for Human Growth* (New York: Van Nostrand-Reinhold, 1971) or R. L. Mosher and D. Purpel, *Supervision: The Reluctant Profession* (Boston: Houghton Mifflin, 1972), for examples of our earlier struggles to move beyond conventional counselor and teacher education.

3. Mosher, R. L. and N. A. Sprinthall, "Psychological Education in Secondary Schools" in *American Psychologist* (25, 1970), pp. 911-924.

4. A portion of this discussion was presented by the second author at the Phi Delta Kappa Research Symposium, University of North Carolina, Greensboro, January, 1976.

5. Archambault, R. D., *John Dewey on Education.* (Chicago: University of Chicago Press, 1964), Preface.

6. Archambault, *op. cit.,* p. 4.

7. Archambault, *op. cit.,* p. 7.

8. Mosher and Sprinthall, *op. cit.*

9. Archambault, *op. cit.,* p. 9.

10. *Ibid.*

11. Cremin, L., *The Transformation of the American School.* (New York: Knopf, 1961).

12. Archambault, *op. cit.,* p. 10.

13. Personal communication from Robert Beck, Regents Professor, University of Minnesota, 1977.

14. Archambault, *op cit.,* p. 10.

15. See the following special issues of journals for recent research: *Counselor Education and Supervision* (14, 4, 1975), *The Counseling Psychologist* (6, 4, 1977), and *The Personnel and Guidance Journal* (52, 4, 1974).

16. Friere, P., *Pedagogy of the Oppressed.* (New York: Herder and Herder, 1970).

Promoting Interpersonal and Moral Growth in Elementary Schools

Robert D. Enright

The cross-age training study to be described in this paper was initiated to increase children's level of social cognitive development. The basic rationale of the study comes from Mosher and Sprinthall's[1] observations that teachers either knowingly or unknowingly specifically influence children's social cognitive development. The present study is a conscious effort to enhance such development using Piaget's[2] cognitive developmental theory as the theoretical foundation. More specifically, the present focus is on interpersonal conceptions from Selman's theory,[3] which can be defined as an ordered sequence of thought about feelings, self-knowledge, personality traits and interpersonal relationships. Because the study of interpersonal conceptions as Selman defines it is relatively new, there is little information about the levels available in the literature. In fact, one of the major omissions in various developmental schema such as the theories of Piaget, Kohlberg, and Flavell, has been the absence of a framework which defines how a person structures and understands the nature of relationships in an interpersonal domain. Therefore, before the training program is described, Selman's framework for stages or levels of interpersonal conceptions will be discussed.

LEVELS OF INTERPERSONAL CONCEPTIONS

Selman's description of interpersonal conceptions encompasses six levels. Within each level, the conceptions are divided into the four catergories of subjectivity, self-awareness, personality, and relationships.

Level *zero* is characterized by a "physical" understanding of the world in that the child does not attribute an internal quality to emotions. Feelings are on people's faces. That is, if someone is smiling, then he/she is happy. Self-awareness involves a physical concept of self, but not a psychological understanding. Personality attributes are determined by skin color or sex. For example, a child reasoning on level zero, when asked, "What kind of a person is Johnny?", may respond, "He's a boy." Friends are those people who give things to the child or who live near him/her. Of two or more people in a relationship, the child's focus is on the self.

At level *one*, the concept of subjectivity, or an understanding of the internal quality of feelings begins to emerge. Also emerging here is an awareness of subjective differences between the self and others and a description of the context specificity of personality, such as, "He is a boy who wants a puppy now." If, in a dyad, one person is satisfied, then the two are friends. Note that it is not always the self who must be satisfied.

Level *two* subjectivity is marked by the awareness of two or more emotions occurring at the same time within one person. For instance, the child may say, "Johnny can feel sad that he lost his old dog and happy that he got the new one." In the self-awareness category, awareness of facades, or the hiding of feelings, is understood for the first time. Personality is still described in context specific concrete terms, but it now takes on an interpersonal component. For instance, a child may say, "Johnny is a boy who wants his friends to think that he doesn't want a new puppy." The most significant accomplishment in the relationship category is the development of reciprocity.

Level *three* subjectivity characterizes feelings as "mixed." For example, the same situation can be seen as producing multiple emotions. Using the level two example, Johnny may

Robert D. Enright

not only feel happy about getting a new dog, but he might have mixed feelings about it because it could remind him of his old dog. Awareness of self is on a continuum from superficial to deep. That is, the child takes into account surface appearances, underlying feelings, and even quantitatively deeper feelings. Relations are viewed on a time continuum in which a good friend is someone the child has gotten to know gradually. Generally, elementary age children can be classified in Selman's Levels 1 to 3.

Level *four* is characterized by the awareness of qualitative levels of subjectivity, self-awareness, personality, and relationships. For instance, the child may be aware of the conscious, preconscious, and subconscious existence of thoughts and feelings. The child now believes that no one can know himself/herself entirely. He/she also believes that subconscious as well as conscious systems influence personality. Relationships are seen as qualitatively distinct, in that the child may be superficial friends with some individuals and exceptionally close friends with others. A person would ordinarily have to be capable of formal operations cognitively in order to process differences between such objective/subjective conceptions of interpersonal functioning.

On Level *five*, a person characterizes persons in terms of their relationships. The unique interactions that are formed between persons A and B and those between A and C bring out different characteristics of person A within the two relationships. For example, the child may observe that friend A acts "bravely" in front of his/her friends and "shyly" with the teacher. The discrepancy is resolved by studying the relationships. The child might conclude that his/her friend is really very unsure of him/herself and this quality manifests itself differently in A's different relationships. Usually, it is not until a person is well into adolescence and has developed the use of formal operations that such a complex process of interpersonal functioning is possible. A more complete description of the levels can be found in Selman.[3]

DESIGN ISSUES

Subjects

Twenty-four children, twelve male and twelve female, from the sixth-grade class of a traditional elementary school in Minneapolis served as subjects. The subjects' ages ranged from 10.7 to 12.4 years at the beginning of the study. Only those children whose parents gave written permission to take part in the study were included. The school is one of five alternative schools comprising a school district. The parents, therefore, chose the traditional emphasis for their children. The population is heterogeneous, but is primarily lower-middle and middle class.

Procedure

A randomized pretest-posttest design was used. Thirty subjects comprised the initial subject pool. The sample was stratified by sex, and twelve males and twelve females were randomly chosen from each group. Six males and six females were then randomly chosen for the experimental condition. The other six males and six females served as the control group. The experimental group took part in a cross-age teaching program in which the sixth-grade pupils learned to lead small group discussions with first-graders. The content focus of the small group discussions was provided by the Guidance Associates Filmstrips on moral dilemmas for elementary age children, plus other appropriate stories. The control group received no training. The experimentals met twice a week for approximately forty-five minutes each time, once to lead the dilemma discussion groups with the first-graders (the cross-age session), and once with the trainers to discuss their experiences as discussion leaders (the reflection session). Two adult supervisors, one male and one female, conducted the reflection sessions and supervised, along with the first-grade teacher, the cross-age sessions. Both supervisors had prior

Robert D. Enright

experience with children's groups as well as an understanding of cognitive developmental theory. Within the experimental group, each subject chose a partner with whom he or she co-led the discussions with the first-graders during the cross-age sessions. Each pair, comprising a total of six groups, had four or five first-graders in the group. The training program lasted for twenty-two weeks. A cross-age program was thought best for training because the children could then think about actual interactions between themselves and the first-graders. The "real world" learning may lead to more relevant and, therefore, easier learning of interpersonal conceptions.

Thus, the over-all instructional format consisted of a series of components which are typical of programs designed a-round the so-called deliberate psychological education for-mat. The pupils in the experimental class learn from real ex-perience in a practicum, conducting small group discussions with the first-graders. The pupils also systematically examine that experience in a seminar with their peers and a supervisor each week. The pupils are helped to increase their specific teaching skills but, more importantly, are also aided to ex-amine their own role performance, how they understand the nature of first-grade children, issues of discipline, of helping, etc. In this way they have an opportunity to learn more about themselves and other children through a significant role-taking experience.

Methods for Increasing Development

Four basic methods were employed by the supervisors to bring about an increase in level of interpersonal conceptions for the experimental group. The methods were as follows:

1) In order to present a lesson to the first-graders, the sixth graders selected storybooks or filmstrips which would serve as the lesson for any given week. The trainers would have the sixth-graders explore the feelings, personalities and relationships of the characters so that they would be better able to teach.

2) Once the children began to explore the interpersonal qualities of a story character, the trainers would attempt to increase the level of a child's conception by asking questions which were one level above the child's current reasoning level. For example, suppose the child said, "I think Mary (a story character) would be sad if she climbed the tree to save the kitten because she promised her dad she wouldn't climb trees." Such a conception is probably Level 1 because the child seems to be aware of internal qualities of feelings. Since a Level 2 concept of subjectivity involves focusing on two or more emotions, the trainer may ask, "Is it possible that Mary might feel sad *and* happy at the same time about climbing the tree?"

3) The third method focused on the actual interactions between the sixth and first-graders after the cross-age sessions. Instead of asking about Mary, the story character, the trainer may ask, "How did Frank (a first-grader) feel when you yelled at him to be quiet?" Or, the trainer may ask a relationship question, such as, "How do you get along with the first-graders when you yell at them?" After the response, the trainer would usually ask a question which required a higher level answer than the previous one to induce more complex thoughts in the child.

4) The final method did not deal with inducing higher level responses, but dealt with discrepancies between a child's thoughts and actions. For example, Barbara would usually say that if she is good to the first-graders, they are good to her. The response appears to be Level 2 in the relationship category because of the reciprocal implications. Yet, Barbara continued to yell in order to quiet her group of first graders. She did not seem to be acting on the reciprocity that she saw as necessary for adequate group functioning. By pointing out her discrepancies of thought and action to her, the trainers were attempting to have her action become more in line with her thoughts. Once this occurred (that is, the yelling stopped), the trainers would attempt method three,

above, by having Barbara reflect on her newly acquired reciprocal behavior. For a more detailed description of the training methods, see Enright.[4]

Instruments

The following five measures were chosen to evaluate the intervention: Selman's interpersonal conceptions measure, Carroll's moral judgment test,[5] Shure and Spivack's social problem-solving task,[6] Flavell, Botkin, Fry, Wright, and Jarvis' referential communication task II B,[7] and WISC-R vocabulary. Selman's was the measure of direct effect while the moral judgment test was chosen as an indirect effect because of the theoretical relationship between the constructs of interpersonal conceptions and moral judgment. Both social problem-solving and referential communication were chosen to measure the limits of the intervention since neither are theoretically related to the stage constructs of interpersonal and moral conceptions. Both social problem solving and referential communication require quantitative responses for higher scores in that the more the child says, the higher the score. WISC-R vocabulary was included because of the possible relationship of interpersonal and moral abilities with verbal ability. Each instrument is briefly described below.

To measure interpersonal conceptions, the experimenter presents to the child a filmstrip about a boy, Mike, who has lost his dog. Mike's friends must decide whether to buy him a new dog or not. The child is then questioned with a standard set of questions about the interpersonal qualities of the filmstrip characters. Clinical probing and followup questions are also used. The measure assesses reasoning in the categories of subjectivity, self-awareness, personality, and relations. In the present study, each response that was scorable was assigned a stage number (1-6). The responses were then classified into one of the four content categories. Means were derived for each category and the total score represented the mean of the four category means.

The moral judgment measure is based on Kohlberg's six levels.[8] After a moral dilemma is read to the child, he/she is presented with ten reasons for either acting or not acting in the moral situation. Four dilemmas are presented. Two reasons per dilemma are represented at each of the moral levels one through five. The scoring consists of a four-point scale, from one point for accepting the reason to four points for rejecting the reason. The scale measures the extent to which a child will reject a lower stage of reason for solving a dilemma. The child receives a score at each moral stage one through five.

The social problem-solving measure consists of six stories about hypothetical problems which children must verbally solve. The experimenter reads the beginning and end of the story and the child is asked to "fill in" the middle. For example, in one story the character has no money but wants to buy his/her mother a present for her birthday. The story ends with the character giving a present to the mother on her birthday. The measure assesses the extent to which the child can plan step-by-step means to reach a desired goal. One point is given for every mean toward reaching the goal, obstacle anticipated, or time notation used by the subject.

In referential communication, the subject is presented with a series of geometric forms which must be verbally described to another individual who cannot see the display. The purpose is to determine the extent to which the child can take into account the needs of the listener by formulating an accurate communication of the object. Zero to four points are given for various levels of accuracy in describing the shape's presence, size, position, and color.

In WISC-R vocabulary, the child is presented with words of increasing difficulty until he/she misses five in a row. All measures except WISC-R vocabulary were given at pretest and posttest. WISC-R vocabulary was given at posttest only. All measures were individually administered, except for mor-

Robert D. Enright

al judgment, which was group administered to ten students at a time.

Predictions

Given the interrelationships between measures as described in the above section, the following outcomes were predicted:

The experimental group would show higher ability than the controls in: (a) interpersonal conceptions, (b) stage one moral judgment, and (c) stage two moral judgment. Because of the relationship between age and stage in moral judgment, one would not expect much improvement beyond the lower stages.[8] The criteria for acceptance of the predictions were significant posttest differences between groups favoring the experimentals.

There were no predicted differences between the groups in: (a) Kohlberg's stage three, four or five, (b) referential communication, (c) social problem-solving, or (d) vocabulary. No significant differences between groups at posttest will be the criteria used here.

Results

All measures, with the exception of referential communication, were found reliable for the present sample. Please see Enright for that data.[4]

To examine treatment outcomes, two-way analyses of variance between groups were first performed on the pretest measures. There were no pretest differences in treatment condition between groups, no sex differences, and no interaction effects for any of the measures. *Table I* presents the means and F ratios for each of the Selman categories. Posttest analyses of variance indicated significant treatment differences favoring the experimentals for the interpersonal conceptions category of subjectivity, for the self-awareness category, for the personality category, for the relationship category, and for the interpersonal conceptions total score.

Table I

INTERPERSONAL CONCEPTIONS
(Selman's Stages: Pretest-Posttest Scores)

	E Group N=12 (6M, 6F)			C Group N=12 (6M, 6F)		
	Pre	Post	F	Pre	Post	F
Subjectivity	2.07	3.01	6.36 <.02	2.17	2.29	N.S.
Self-Aware-ness	2.04	2.92	11.29 <.004	2.11	2.18	N.S.
Personality	2.17	3.46	19.76 <.002	2.32	2.31	N.S.
Relation-ships	1.92	3.13	11.67 <.004	2.12	2.14	N.S.

Level 2 = Concrete thinking, perception of two or more feelings, beginning of reciprocity.

Level 3 = Beginning of abstractions, perception of multiple emotions, distinguish between surface and more in-depth feelings, greater time perspective.

In the area of moral judgment, a more indirect assessment of the dependent variable, *Table II* presents the posttest mean scores and F ratios. At each stage, two sets of reasons are presented and the pupil is asked to either accept or reject those reasons. Answers are scored on a four-point continuum, complete acceptance (=1) to complete rejection (=4).

Table II
KOHLBERG MORAL JUDGMENT SCORES
(Posttest Means)

Stage	E Group N=12	C Group N=12	F
One	17.2	13.2	4.21 <.05
Two	17.3	14.0	4.67 <.05
Three	15.2	12.1	4.28 <.05
Four	15.1	12.6	N.S.
Five	15.1	12.4	N.S.

(The higher the score the more likely the pupil is to reject thinking at that stage.)

The results indicated that the pupils in the E group showed a consistent tendency to reject relatively low-level stage reasoning (Kohlberg Stages One through Three) when compared to the control group scores.

On the other measures of effect there were no significant differences between the two groups on measures of social problem solving (Shure and Spivack), referential communication (Flavell, et. al.) or on the WISC-R vocabulary test.

There were no sex differences found for any of the measures on the posttest analyses.

Implications

The present study was designed to test out the possible effects of a carefully developed program designed to teach elementary age pupils how to teach and understand their younger peers. As is noted and extensively documented elsewhere in this issue, peer and cross-age teaching programs and action-learning plans have been increasingly popular in the last decade. All this in spite of the lack of documentation as to impact or effect of such programs. Indeed, one could almost worry about the possible exploitation of children as a cheap source of instructional help if so little is known concerning such programs.

The present study is essentially the first controlled investigation employing a randomized design and balanced for sex differences. With twenty-four sixth-grade pupils equally divided by sex, one-half were assigned to the Experimental Curriculum, while the others simply experienced school as usual. The curriculum was a highly structured intervention. The Trainers worked in small seminar-like groups (N=5 or 6) and asked a series of indirect and probing questions designed to help the sixth-graders understand the teaching process themselves, and how younger children think and feel. The seminars met each week for twenty-two weeks to examine the cross-age teaching. Thus, it was an intensive experience and a carefully supervised balance between a practicum and a seminar for the sixth-graders. It is well to remember that this framework seems to be the central component of effective programs: namely, *carefully supervised experience on an ongoing basis. The pace is slow, the experience continuous and connected.*

The results indicated quite clearly that the experimental group, especially on the most direct evaluation of social cognitive development, the Selman scales, demonstrated significant growth toward an increase in mature interpersonal conceptions. The seminar-practicum stimulated the development of an increased sensitivity, understanding a greater complex-

Robert D. Enright

ity in emotions, a greater ability to understand from a variety of viewpoints. The social role-taking perspective increased on an overall basis. In more everyday words, the students in the programs manifested a greater ability to perceive human interactions in non-stereotyped ways.

Although the relationship between stages of interpersonal conception (Selman) and moral judgment (Kohlberg) are not exact, theoretically there should be at least an indirect effect, or necessary but not entirely sufficient relationship, between the two aspects of development. In the current study, the most significant impact was on the stage of interpersonal development. There was, however, a consistent, though less significant, impact on the stage of moral development. The pupils in the experimental group tended to be more definite than the controls in rejecting lower stage thinking. Thus, they were less attracted by thinking at Kohlberg's Stages One, Two, and Three that the "regular" sixth-graders. This, in itself, is a somewhat incomplete finding, since the statistical analysis failed to show the "other side," so to speak. There was no clear positive preference for higher stages by the experimental group. The two findings do, however, suggest that there is an indirect relationship between growth in interpersonal and in moral development.

The lack of significance of the other findings, in general, indicates that such a program does not seem to affect the pupils' vocabulary, their planning orientation or their ability to view geometric shapes from a variety of perspectives. Since none of these aspects of development were necessarily related to the objectives of the curriculum, the lack of significance in these domains support the overall conclusion that the program was targeted to impact the social cognitive development from an interpersonal conception focus.

The next step in social cognitive developmental interventions is to measure children's behavioral interactions in their classroom and playground environments to see if increased social cognitive ability leads to more adequate social interaction, no matter how the latter may be defined. If we are genuinely helping children lead better lives by social cognitive interventions, then it would seem that we should expect to find changes not only in children's responses to our interview questions, but also in the way children solve their day-to-day social problems.

NOTES and REFERENCES

1. Mosher, R. L., and N. A. Sprinthall, "Psychological Education: A Means to Promote Personal Development During Adolescence," in *The Counseling Psychologist,* (2, 1971), pp. 3-82.

2. Piaget, J., "The General Problems of the Psychobiological Development of the Child," in J. M. Tanner, and B. Inhelder (Eds.), *Discussions on Child Development,* Vol. IV. (New York: International Universities Press, 1960).

3. Selman, R. L., *The Development of Interpersonal Relations.* Harvard-Judge Baker Social Reasoning Project, (December, 1974). (Available from: R. L. Selman, Harvard Graduate School of Education, Larsen Hall, Cambridge, Massachusetts 02138).

4. Enright, R. D., *Social Cognitive Development: A Training Model for Intermediate School-Age Children.* (St. Paul, Minnesota: Minnesota State Department of Education, 1977).

5. Carroll, J., *Children's Judgments of Statements Exemplifying Different Moral Stages.* (Unpublished doctoral dissertation, University of Minnesota, 1974).

6. Shure, M. B., and G. Spivack, "Means-Ends Thinking, Adjustment, and Social Class among Elementary School Aged Children," in *Journal of Counseling and Clinical Psychology.* (38, 1972), pp. 348-353.

7. Flavell, J. H., P. Botkin, C. Fry, J. Wright, and P. Jarvis, *The Development of Role-Taking and Communication Skills in Children.* (New York: Wiley, 1968).

8. Kohlberg, L., "Stage and Sequence," in D. A. Goslin (Ed.) *Handbook of Socialization Theory and Research.* (Chicago: Rand McNally, 1969).

Robert D. Enright

Moral Education with Children: An Examination of Related Studies

David E. Stuhr

INTRODUCTION

In the past four years I have sponsored four major dissertations by Counselor Education students at Boston University which evaluated moral education curricula. This research focused on the moral reasoning of pre-adolescent students and early adolescent students. The moral development theory of Lawrence Kohlberg has provided the theoretical base for each of these inquiries.[1] The studies themselves have been conducted in three different school systems, all of which are in principally middle-class suburbs of Boston. To be so closely affiliated with this research, and with the doctoral students who have completed it, has afforded me the opportunity to develop ideas for curricular and theoretical improvements in moral education. The purpose of this article is, therefore, to share my experience and my recommendations with the reader.

THE RESEARCH FINDINGS

It is not my intention to even try to fully share the research of my students. Each of their dissertations justify an independent report. However, as I see it, I can briefly summarize their research and provide some initial integration for their findings.

In 1973 when we began, there was very little reported on moral education, in general, and even less on moral education with elementary and junior high school children, in particular. Blatt's 1970 dissertation had reported success in the use of moral discussions to enhance the moral reasoning of fifth and sixth grade students in a church school.[2] However, at that time, his was the only study in the literature which reported using both pre-adolescents and Kohlberg's developmental hierarchy. Blatt used a moral discussion approach in his study that has become the most often used means of stimulating moral development. He stressed providing students with the opportunity to hear arguments one stage higher than their own. His success is well known. What my students have done is built upon Blatt's experience.

1. The 1974 Dissertation of Patrica Grimes[3]

Patricia Grimes' dissertation reported on research that added two things to Blatt's research: she worked in a public school setting, and she included mothers in one of her treatment groups. Her research compared a group of fifth and sixth grade students, a group of fifth and sixth grade students and their mothers, and a group of untreated fifth and sixth grade students. The treatment Grimes used was composed of three, sequential phases: (1) learning how to discuss moral issues; (2) in-depth discussions of moral dilemmas; and (3) the enactment of morality plays.

The group composed of students and their mothers also received three pre-treatment sessions for the students' mothers. These sessions were devoted to exposing the mothers to moral development and moral education. The concepts of moral reasoning, development, stages and dilemma discussion were presented and discussed. This time served to prepare the mothers for the meetings with their children.

The mother/student group began by discussing dilemmas presented by the leader. These were either taken from avail-

David E. Stuhr

able materials or were created by the leader. The course then shifted, and the participants read a children's novel, **Sounder**. The members of the group were asked to find and discuss the moral dilemmas in that story. Next, participants, particularly the children, wrote dilemmas. These were then presented and discussed. The group finished by enacting moral dilemma vignettes that had been written by Grimes. For the most part, the children played the roles in these vignettes. All of the material used was designed, or selected, to be appropriate for fifth and sixth graders.

Grimes' results were striking. By the end of the treatment, children in the mother/student group had moved one-half a stage. Children in the student-only group moved only one-third a stage. Children in the control group, however, changed not at all.

Grimes' groups of fifth and sixth graders began at Stage 2. For example: only one student in each of the two treatment groups tested at Stage 3 before being exposed to her treatment. However, at the end of the treatment, all but two students in the mother/student group were testing at Stage 3.

The inclusion of students' mothers had powerful effects. Grimes reported that she felt this during the course of the treatment, and the results confirmed it. The mothers were able to extend the in-school treatment into the family life of the students. In addition, it appeared that the inclusion of their mothers served to motivate the students to fully participate in the curriculum.

These results of Grimes' research led us to ask many questions. Since the group that included students' mothers was significantly more successful than the group that included only students, we wondered if we could do anywhere near as well with a curriculum that was developed for use in a more conventional elementary school classroom. We also wondered what would be the impact of including fathers in the treatment. We even speculated on whether parents could be trained without including the students in the training at all.

2. The 1976 Dissertation of Diana Paolitto[4]

Diana Paolitto's dissertation reported on the next study, which was conducted in a classroom setting and examined a curriculum that highlighted perspective taking. Her study was implemented in a Kindergarten through Grade 8 elementary school that was part of a predominantly middle-class school system, but whose students were from working-class families. The students in her study were eighth graders who were socially different from the fifth and sixth graders in Grimes' earlier study, but the students in Paolitto's group were at approximately the same level of moral reasoning as the students in Grimes' groups. The students in both studies were at Stage 2 in moral reasoning, although Grimes' students were from upper-middle-class families while Paolitto's students were from lower-to-middle class families.

Paolitto's curriculum treatment was twenty weeks in length, and was rich in opportunities for the students to vicariously share in the experience others had had with moral dilemmas in their own lives. The treatment itself included three phases: (1) understanding moral dilemmas; (2) communicating moral dilemmas; and (3) learning about moral dilemmas faced by people in the community. This third and last phase required twelve weeks, and was the focal point of the course. During this phase, selected adults were invited into the classroom to discuss with the students the moral dilemmas they experienced in their own work.

Paolitto began her curriculum treatment with instruction in contrasting moral decisions with common decisions which do not include a value component. This first phase included a standard exposure to moral dilemmas and the discussion of such dilemmas. After the students were able to participate in these discussions, role play and dilemmas designed by the students were incorporated into the classroom experience. These parts of Paolitto's course were very closely related to Grimes' treatments.

The final and longest third phase (twelve weeks) included

David E. Stuhr

student interviews of school personnel, and other adults from their community. These often were group interviews. Then the class developed dilemmas for the school people. These discussions would begin with the student related dilemmas, but they often re-focused on the dilemmas that were offered by the adults from their own current array of problems. The people from the community presented their own dilemmas, and the discussions with these adults began and ended with that focus. All of the interviews conducted during this third phase were designed to maximize the opportunity for students to take, and to comprehend, the perspectives of the adults being interviewed.

Paolitto taught the course herself, as Grimes had done earlier. However, in Paolitto's study, the students were taught in a regularly scheduled health class. The only novel aspect of the course she taught was its content. That is, the students in her study were not in a special place, nor were they in a special group.

In her study, Paolitto measured both moral reasoning and perspective taking. Significant changes, compared to an *intact comparison* group, were achieved only on the moral reasoning measure. This result is interesting, since Grimes had speculated that perspective taking was an important element of a curriculum for students who were principally reasoning at Stage 2. The work of Paolitto suggests that this is so, but it raises questions about whether perspective taking is as large a contributor to moving from Stage 2 to Stage 3 in moral reasoning as we had hypothesized. For example: her experimental group began at almost the exact average stage as had Grimes' experimental groups - - only one of Paolitto's seventeen students tested at Stage 3. Yet, at the conclusion of the treatment, only two additional students had joined that one student at a tested Stage 3 of moral reasoning.

Paolitto's study added to the evidence that we could change the moral reasoning of pre-adolescents and early adolescents. Still, her experimental group changed only slightly less than one-third of a stage, which was less than Grimes' students-only group had changed. It is difficult to interpret this difference between the two studies, of course, because the groups did differ in age, socio-economic status, and in setting. One must remember that the students in Grimes' groups were volunteers, while Paolitto's students were enrolled in a required course. If nothing else, these differences point out the difficulties in establishing a line of research within the context of a training program.

However, Paolitto's and Grimes' studies do complement each other, and together they have raised important research questions. Certainly the evidence that educationally significant growth could be stimulated in the context of a *regular* classroom was marginal. Also, the potential impact of a course which stressed perspective taking remained moot. What seemed to be needed was additional research with middle- class and upper-middle- class students, before we attempted to examine the effectiveness of this kind of curricular treatment with other student populations.

3. The 1977 Dissertation of Louise Rundle[5]

Louise Rundle's dissertation reported on her development and testing of a fifth grade moral education curriculum. In her study, Rundle compared experimentally three groups: (1) an intervention group in which the daily events of the classroom were used as the content for moral discussions; (2) an intervention group in which the traditional approach of leader-developed dilemmas were used as the content for moral discussions; and (3) a control group in which no intervention was used at all. The two intervention groups occurred in an elementary school in a middle class to upper-middle class suburban school system to the West of Boston. Each intervention was of twelve weeks duration, and each intervention group met once or twice each week. The total moral education curriculum developed by Rundle required twenty-nine hours of instruction.

The intervention group which capitalized on the use of

David E. Stuhr

classroom events promoted the students' involvement in decision-making that was related to classroom and school matters. Because of the very nature of Rundle's interventions, it was necessary to include the regular classroom teacher as a co-teacher of the experimental moral education curricula. However, the impact of Rundle's treatment reached beyond the specific instructional hours devoted to the intervention, much as had happened with Grimes' mother/student group. Unfortunately, the traditional moral education intervention was conducted in a classroom where the regular teacher was perceived by the students as being authoritarian. As a result, the comparison between the two competing forms of moral education curricula are subject to many limitations.

Rundle's main treatment (i.e., the intervention that used the events of the classroom as the content for moral education) was designed to offer fifth graders an opportunity to do four things: to discuss moral dilemmas, to take the role of others, to make classroom decisions, and to modify classroom rules and conditions. The last two of these opportunities were those which were unique to her *main* experimental treatment.

The classroom decision-making component included such issues as talking back to the teacher, talking in the class, and having candy for snacks. While none of these issues are earth-shaking matters, they happened to be the issues about which the students were concerned. As this class became more proficient in decision-making, a general methodology emerged which most often led to consensus. First, the class would discuss a problem and highlight the issues involved. Then, in small groups the students would debate the issues and arrive at a small group resolution. Finally, the small groups would report and the class as a whole would work toward a consensus.

Only Rundle's *main* treatment led to improved moral reasoning. The intervention group that used her main treatment improved one-half a stage: they moved from a low Stage 2 to a very solid Stage 2. While the inability to separate teacher effects from curriculum effects in Rundle's study does interfere with our ability to interpret these results, they do add to our understanding of moral education. For the first time, Rundle's study showed that practically significant growth in moral reasoning was stimulated within the context of a regular classroom. This finding, plus the evident implications of developing a moral action environment within a classroom, are major contributions to our understanding of moral education.

4. The 1978 Dissertation of Robert Azrak[6]

Robert Azrak's dissertation reported on his study of the impact of training parents of junior high school students to be, themselves, moral educators. His study was an outgrowth of the earlier work of Grimes and the work reported in Stanley's dissertation.[7] Stanley, while working with parents and adolescents, had demonstrated that affecting parenting procedures could produce changes in students' moral reasoning. Although Stanley was interested in stimulating students' moral reasoning, he never worked directly with them. Azrak's curriculum, on the other hand, parallels those used in the other studies that have been reported here. He created a curriculum that introduced parents to moral development theory, taught them how to lead moral discussions and, then, finished by having the parents apply their new understandings and skills to their own everyday discipline problems with their pre-teenagers.

In the context of Azrak's treatment, parents dealt with issues such as property, contracts, and punishment. The main, recurring theme of his treatment involved parents understanding their children (from a developmental perspective) and, so, coping with them (from a perspective of reason and equality, rather than from a perspective of power). After all, it is not easy to relate to a developmental inferior as an equal. It is doubly difficult if that person happens to be your own child. Yet, the power parents have is illusive and, it seems,

David E. Stuhr

always diminishing.

Frankly, Azrak's results were only marginally good. The students whose parents had received training improved only one-fifth of a stage. While the results were statistically significant, their practical significance appears to lie in the hope that trained parents will continue to act as moral educators. If that should prove to be so, then we could anticipate continued growth on the part of the students whose parents had been trained. Follow-up testing by Stanley suggests that the hope is not vain.[7]

SOME IMPLICATIONS FOR CURRICULUM

The four studies by Grimes, Paolitto, Rundle and Azrak that have been described suggest that children and early adolescents respond to most moral education curricula. Educationally significant gains in moral reasoning do occur, especially when the experiences involve the students' lives, and when the utility of the experience itself is apparent to the students. Relatively short-term interventions are quite successful, especially when the experiences are ones that reach beyond the curriculum. Perspective taking does seem to be an important curriculum variable, but it seems to be critically important to join such experiences with other decision-making experiences.

Our findings seem to support the development of an educational environment in which youngsters are empowered to participate in the making of important decisions. To simply discuss quite hypothetical issues may be losing its power. The gift of the franchise seems to be much more effective. The student who has a vote in the classroom, or in the home, appears to be the student most likely to grow in moral reasoning.

Our students have moved from approximately a Stage 2 level of moral reasoning to a Stage 3 level of moral reasoning. Whether educational interventions similar to those we have developed will be successful with students reasoning at the higher stages, or who are generally socially more sophisticated, is currently being tested by Mosher and Sullivan, among others.[8] But there seems to be little reason to doubt that the ages from ten through thirteen are profitable years for moral education. Therefore, we look for colleagues who will join in a search for better programs, for we are convinced that this is an important work.

SOME THEORETICAL IMPLICATIONS

As was stated at the outset, our research has focused on moral reasoning. In most of the studies that have been described, additional dependent variables were included in the studies. For example, Rundle used a measure of cooperation to examine the impact of her treatment.[5] Her main treatment, which incorporated the use of classroom experiences as the content of moral education, led to significant gains in cooperation.

Our problems in beginning to look at moral action, as well as at moral reasoning, are many. However, all of those problems originate from the lack of a comprehensive theory. At the present, we have no theory which directs our inquiry into moral action. Social learning theory, for example, speaks to the factors which control moral action. But there is no theory which fully integrates reasoning and action.

Our research indirectly suggests that reasoning and action are closely related. We find that students can act themselves into new ways of thinking, as well as think themselves into new ways of acting.[5] Yet, when we examine moral action, we are too often forced into studying *ad hoc* behaviors. For example, we have no theoretical answer to such basic questions as why one should choose to study cooperation or, conversely, why one should not choose cooperation but some other behavior. The theoretical vacuum persists.

As I observe the movement of moral educators like Kohlberg and Mosher to the development of moral environments,[9,10] and as I observe the readiness of social learning theorists like Mahoney to incorporate cognition into both

David E. Stuhr

their theories and their research,[11] I see opportunities for research which will truly integrate the several aspects of moral behavior (i.e., thoughts and emotions, as well as actions). For the moral educator, this need for integration is critical. The educator *qua* educator must both manage the educational environment and, as well, justify moral education programs. Both of those tasks cry out for information about moral action, especially its relationship to other categories of social behavior. However, to date, no existing theory has been particularly effective in focusing and directing inquiry into the full range of moral behavior. It is time for those of us in the field to broaden our perspectives, and to cast aside our theoretical prejudices. Much is to be gained by dialogue across theoretical communities.

REFERENCES

1. Kohlberg, L. "Stage and Sequence: the Cognitive Developmental Approach to Socialization," in D. Goslin (Ed.) *Handbook of Socialization Theory and Research.* (New York: Rand McNally, 1969.)

2. Blatt, M. *Studies on the Effects of Classroom Discussions Upon Children's Moral Development.* (Unpublished doctoral dissertation, University of Chicago, 1970.)

3. Grimes, P. *Teaching Moral Reasoning to Eleven Year Olds and Their Mothers: Means of Promoting Moral Development.* (Unpublished doctoral dissertation, Boston University, 1974. Xerox Order No. 7402433.)

4. Paolitto, D. *Role-taking Opportunities for Early Adolescents: A Program in Moral Education.* (Unpublished doctoral dissertation, Boston University, 1976. Xerox Order No. 7611829.)

5. Rundle, L. *The Stimulation of Moral Development in the Elementary School and the Cognitive Examination of Social Experience: A Fifth Grade Study.* (Unpublished doctoral dissertation, Boston University, 1977. Xerox Order No. 7721675.)

6. Azrak, R. *Training Fathers and Mothers in Psychological Discipline Strategies: A Curriculum to Effect Attitudes Toward Childbearing and the Moral Development of Early Adolescents.* (Unpublished doctoral dissertation, Boston University, 1978.)

7. Stanley, S. *Curriculum to Affect the Moral Atmosphere of the Family and the Moral Development of Adolescence.* (Unpublished doctoral dissertation, Boston University, 1976.)

8. Mosher, R. L., and P. Sullivan. "A Curriculum for Adolescents in Moral Education," in *Focus on Guidance* (1974).

9. Kohlberg, L., E. Wasserman, and N. Richardson. "The Just Community School: The Theory and the Cambridge Cluster School Experiment," in *Collected Papers on Moral Development and Moral Education.* ((Vol. 2, 1975, Mimeo.)

10. Mosher, R. L. "A Funny Thing Happened on the Way to Curriculum Development," in H. Peters and R. Aubrey (Eds.) *Guidance: Strategies and Techniques.* (Denver, Colorado: Love Publishing Co., 1975).

11. Mahoney, M. J. *Cognition and Behavior Modification.* (Cambridge, Massachusetts: Ballinger Publishing Co., 1974).

David E. Stuhr

Students as Teachers: Role Taking as a Means of Promoting Psychological and Ethical Development During Adolescence

Philip V. Cognetta
Norman A. Sprinthall

INTRODUCTION

Although there is a growing body of literature available describing the use of school pupils as tutors/teachers, there are few substantial conclusions, especially in the area of the psychological impact upon the student as tutor. Indeed, several current reviewers of the cross-age teaching literature, Allen,[1] Paolitto,[2] Bloom,[3] have singled out the personal development of the tutor as an area where additional research is needed.

Historically, the use of students as teachers is certainly not a new phenomenon. Anecdotal accounts from this country's "little red school houses," as well as the more formal Lancaster system in 19th Century England, attest to the historical base for such programs. Indeed, Paolitto's comprehensive review presents written evidence as far back as Quentilian in the 1st Century A.D. In spite of this long tradition, however, there is much that is unknown concerning such programs.

RATIONALE

The main focus of the current investigation, as in that conducted by Enright, is upon the effects of cross-age teaching on the tutors themselves. Generally, most of the research available, although of uneven quality, does tend to establish that tutees benefit from the process (especially in areas of school achievement). This outcome has been supported by numerous studies with pupils from different socio-economic backgrounds, ethnic and racial characteristics. Allen, et. al.,[4] conclude, "It is clear . . . other racial and social class groups produce significant academic improvement when tutoring children of the same race and status."

What is not clear from these studies is the psychological/self concept effects upon the tutors themselves. This is a particularly salient question, given the upsurge of interest in so-called "action-learning programs" recommended by such eminent educators as Ralph Tyler,[5] and the newest Coleman Report.[6] Again, Allen, et. al., note that there is little indication of what type of tutor is effective; however, their definition of "effective" is ambiguous.[7] Some studies indicate low achievers as tutors benefit. Others are equivocal. Paolitto notes that much of the tutor-outcome research is riddled with cultural bias. Tutors' "adjustment" improved, the "trouble-makers" became "serious," etc. Anecdotal comments abound, revealing an undercurrent of socialization goals. Tutors became more orderly in school, "better citizens," neater in appearance . . .[8] The school adjustment ideology seemed to Paolitto and others as a blatantly embarrassing example of a cultural stereotype. The cross-age programs could be enlisted in the service of conformity as a primary educational objective. Indeed, she suggests that a major shortcoming of such programs for tutors may be the emphasis on socialization rather than personal and/or psychological development. This also raises the question of whether exploitation is implicit in such programs, namely that pupils-as-teachers become a cheap labor source for tightly budgeted school districts.

THEORETICAL OBJECTIVES

As a result, it seems clear that a useful study is needed of the possible educational/psychological effects of teaching-tutoring programs. The major dependent variable (or outcome focus) of the proposed study would be the educational impact upon the tutor. In order to define the outcome in generalizable educational terms, the present study derived the dependent variables from a cognitive-developmental framework. Based on the original theories of Dewey, Baldwin, and Mead and more recently on the work of Kohlberg, Erikson and Selman, the framework suggests the stimulation of psychological growth in a stage sequence as a deliberate aim of education. Growth can be defined as movement toward more complex aspects of human functioning - - more comprehensive "thinking," the ability to abstract, to perceive others' viewpoints, and to empathize. Also, recent theory and research suggests that such developmental "growth" or psychological maturity can be stimulated (yet not accelerated) through a process of social role-taking experience.

From this perspective, then, teaching adolescents how to instruct other pupils can be thought of as educating them to experience and perform more complex social roles. If such a process is successful in terms of their own increased psychological maturation, then specific types of peer and/or cross-age teaching could be defended as producing significant educational outcomes.

In a most general sense, then, the theoretical objective of the present study, and others in this model, is directly related to the Dewey-Kohlberg view which holds that psychological development is the proper aim of education. This issue is completely presented in the recent article by Kohlberg and Mayer and will not be repeated here.[9] Thus, the objective is not toward healthy adjustment, socialization, acculturation, academic achievement or any conformity variables. Rather, the objective is to stimulate the development of more complex thinking (including ethical and empathic processing) by the high school pupils. If successful, such programs could then be viewed as intrinsically beneficial rather than in socialization and possibly exploitive terms.

Some of the original work by Gartner, Kohler and Riessman (1971)[10] as well as clinical studies by Atkins (1971)[11] and Powell (1970)[12] are the exceptions in the cross-age literature. These studies did focus on psychological development as outcome and provided a base for the current studies. Their results were promising and suggestive yet not definitive.

In order to achieve the objective, a sequenced curriculum was created in which there was a balance between real experience in teaching and a careful and systematic reflection on the meaning of that experience. This will be described in some detail in the following section to illustrate the curriculum design issues. The experience was carefully structured and the reflection was guided.

THE CURRICULUM

The class, an elective in Social Studies, was open to tenth through twelfth grade students as part of the self-registration program of the school. The class was co-taught by a regular member of the teaching staff and the researcher. As an integral part of the curriculum, senior high students taught junior high (sixth to eighth grade) students in small groups on a regular, twice-a-week basis. The junior high students were members of an ungraded special elective class that deals with students' interests and socialization activities.

Format: The seminar-practicum format was employed to provide senior high students with responsible social role-taking opportunities as teachers of junior high students. This format placed the student in a responsible adult role where he or she could experiment by trying out various instructional strategies, confront the new and the unknown, pose questions, formulate hypotheses and seek solutions and, through reflection, reconcile what he or she found as a result of those thoughts. The student was also able to compare those findings with those of other students via significant social interaction.

Practicum: The practicum consisted of students systematically experiencing teaching within each of the major Flanders

Cognetta and Sprinthall

Classroom Interaction Categories[13] utilizing Allen's[14] micro-teaching procedures, beginning by direct teaching in the form of giving directions, students then proceeded to Flanders' indirect teaching categories: asking questions, accepting or using the ideas of students, praising, encouraging, and accepting the feelings of students. Thus, the high schoolers learned each teaching skill of the Flanders System through highly structured class exercises.

The actual teaching experiences focused on the following areas and include the following topics:

   I. *Giving directions* - utilizing appropriate exercises

  II. *Asking questions* - interview format employing a questionnaire designed to illustrate differences in concrete and abstract thinking

 III. *Active listening* - leading a moral dilemma discussion

 IV. *Nonverbal communication* - student designed activity employing nonverbal communication of feelings

  V. *"I" messages* - illustrating the concept of personal power and more productive means of communication; student designed activity to solicit and analyze typical adolescent reactions to "you" messages (Thomas Gorden, Teacher Effectiveness Training)[15]

 VI. *Indirect teaching* - employing interest group activities

 VII. *Indirect teaching* - using moral dilemmas - "First Things," "What Do You Do About Rules?" (Guidance Associates Filmstrips)

Seminar: The seminar portion provided opportunities for additional experiential learning as well as significant social interaction through more traditional instructional procedures. Each lesson to be taught to the junior high students was first experienced in the confines of the senior high class with the students functioning as either learner or instructor. The resources of the group were employed to assess the trial teaching performances and to assist in developing or modifying individual teaching units. Essentially, we followed a modeling procedure outlined by Joyce and Weil.[16] The instructors would demonstrate a particular teaching skill from the Flanders'System, e.g., giving directions. The students would then practice the skill themselves and reverse roles. Then, the students would teach a mini-unit to the junior high pupils.

The seminar also allowed for feedback, debriefing and reflection. Students received feedback by viewing videotapes of their teaching along with peers' verbal critiques. Students also were placed in the responsible role of rating each other's teaching performance on the Flanders'Classroom Interaction System and providing accurate feedback. Thus, they learned to judge their peers in practice teaching and indirectly to examine their own teaching. Class discussions followed individual debriefings. The discussions took the form of reflecting and reporting on the teaching experience. Significant social interaction was elicited by discussions that personalized the readings and pertinent social psychological principles of teaching and learning that were examined (i.e., intrinsic and extrinsic motivation, rewards and punishments, etc.) throughout the course. Readings were selected to illustrate specific instructional principles. In brief the content included:

--Portions of **Dibbs**, by Virginia Axline - to illustrate non-verbal communication

--Portions of **Nigger**, by Dick Gregory - to illustrate the effects of teaching in relation to shame and punishment

--Portions of **Catcher in the Rye**, by J. D. Salinger - to illustrate the negative effects of "you" messages

--Portions of **Educational Psychology: A Developmental Approach**, by R. C. Sprinthall and N. A. Sprinthall - student discipline, teaching and education

--Selected handouts on communication

--**Micro-teaching**, a film featuring Dwight Allen - to examine the components of the teaching process

--**What Do You Think?** - a film featuring David Elkind - to illustrate modes of thinking - intuitive, concrete, abstract

--**Faces on a Barroom Floor** - a Charlie Chaplin film - to illustrate nonverbal communication

CURRICULUM AND DEVELOPMENTAL THEORY

In theoretical terms, the course was designed as a progressive sequence of learning experiences. The students were gradually placed in a more complex social role, that of a teacher. They learned new skills to enhance their new role performance. They also were involved in substantial reciprocal role-taking. In the practice-teaching exercises, for example, they would exchange roles as teacher, pupil, judge, and commentator on the process. Mastering the specific skills or components of the Flanders System, provided them with a framework for the analysis of teaching, as well as the experience from a variety of roles. Thus, the heart of the program for teenagers was the careful development of role-taking and perspective-taking related to the art of teaching. (We should add, as a caution, that the students tend to transfer and generalize this perspective-taking to some of their regular classrooms. Tact and diplomacy are requisite when our teenagers report that some of the regular school teachers employ excessive Y-messages, rely exclusively on Flanders "5," and are inept in understanding a pupil's feelings.) In a developmental sense the seminar-practicum experience was designed to stimulate more complex and empathic role-taking in both the Selman sense of stages of interpersonal conceptions (see Enright's paper in this issue) and in the Kohlberg stage model.

In general, adolescence is a time when teenagers are processing experience at both a Selman and Kohlberg Stage 3. Elkind has noted the ubiquitous nature of the adolescent personal fable, excessive egocentric world view, and reliance and other-directedness.[17] Thus, the need for positive educational experiences specifically tailored to adolescent stage concerns are obvious and have been extensively commented upon else-where by Mosher and Sprinthall.[18] Suffice to say, then, that the role-taking involved in teaching appears as a significant mechanism to stimulate the growth of more mature and complex stage functioning by teenagers. The shorthand way of describing this is to note that the developmental objective would be to stimulate growth toward Stage 4 on both the Kohlberg-Selman and Loevinger[19] frameworks. At those stages the individual has a greater inner-directedness, employs abstract rules and differentiates emotions in self and others. In an Erik Erikson sense, the adolescent's ego becomes more integrated, responsive and responsible as an indicator of increased maturity.

RESULTS: THE EFFECTS OF THE PROGRAM

To measure the impact of the program, a design was created to assess the effect upon the psychological and ethical stage of development of the high school pupils. An earlier year long program by Mosher and Sullivan had empirically demonstrated positive outcomes on both the general level of developmental functioning (based on Loevinger's test of Ego Development) and on the level of moral development, using the Kohlberg scores. Since their program was substantially longer than a regular high school course, we designed the present study to test out the same variables over the period of the more usual 12-14 week high school schedule. Also, the curriculum content of the present class was not so directly oriented to teaching Kohlberg's stages to the high school students. Thus, if there was a shift in ego and ethical level we would be on more solid ground in claiming that effects were derived from the role-taking and perspective-taking rather than knowledge of the theory (at least for the moral development scores).

Table I and *Table II* indicate that the Experimentals improved both in Loevinger Stage Score and on the Rest **Defining Issues Test** of moral development. The compar-

Table I

LOEVINGER EGO DEVELOPMENT SCORES
for both a Pretest and Posttest of Experimentals vs. Controls

Groups and Numbers/ Group	Pretest	Posttest	Value of t (one tailed)	Level of Significance
Experimental Class (N=17)	5.29	6.05	3.49	less than .005
Comparison Class (N=26)	4.50	4.46		n.s.

NOTE: The Loevinger Stage Scores were transformed to a 1-10 Scale according to the following convention.

Loevinger's Stage Scores	1	2	Δ	Δ3	3	3-4	4	4-5	5	6
Transformed Stage Scores	1	2	3	4	5	6	7	8	9	10

N.B.: Since random assignment was not possible, separate correlated t Tests were performed.

ison classes (since in a strict sense, these were in-tact regular classes in social studies) showed no growth on either instrument. The increase on the Loevinger, in stage specific terms, was movement from Stage 3 (5.0) to Stage 3-4 (6.0). At Stage 3, a person functions largely in accordance with other-directedness, and is field dependent, (constantly checking out what "the leading crowd" is doing). All of Elkind's classic definitions of adolescent personal mythology and fables fit this stage.[20] It is a stage involved with attempting to please all significant reference groups, of following the most obvious stimulus and possessing little ego strength.[21]

Table II

REST'S MORAL DEVELOPMENT SCORES
for both a Pretest and Posttest of Experimentals vs. Controls

Groups and Numbers/ Group	Pretest [a]	Posttest [a]	Value of t (one tailed)	Level of Significance
Experimental Class (N=15)[b]	28.6%	35.1%	2.13	less than .05
Comparison Class (N=16)[b]	38.4%	37.5%		n.s.

[a] The Pretest and Posttest Rest moral development scores are reported as the percent (%) of his Principled Thought Scale (i.e., combined Stage 5 and Stage 6), although the value of t was computed on the normalized raw scores.

[b] The sample size varies according to the numbers of usable pre/post protocols available from the two groups.

On the other hand, Stage 3-4 is the beginning of inner-directedness and conscientiousness. There is an increase in differentiation of perception both in thoughts and feelings of self and others. The thinking process is more complex and possibilities and probabilities (in the Elkind "as if" sense) increase.

Similarly, the increase in Rest score indicates that the class improved in its ability to process ethical questions more in accord with principled thinking than by social convention (Stage 3) or instrumental hedonism (Stage 2).[22]

Unobtrusive and clinical evidence was also consistent with these empirical results. Posttest interviews with the students contained many comments and perceptions as to how the students themselves experienced the class. Although by itself such interview data would not be substantial, in concert with

Cognetta and Sprinthall

the so-called "hard" evidence it is instructive. Generally, the students whose scores showed "growth" made congruent comments: e.g., "I really learned to take risks," or "I can talk with teachers and my parents now more as an equal," or "I felt important and competent in teaching others," or "It was scary at times, but I learned I could do it," or "It helped me see things from the other side of the desk," or "At first all I saw was a bunch of grubby 7th graders, then I began to remember how awful it is to be that small in a big junior-senior high."

Further, all the students would highly recommend the class to their friends and wished to continue in other similar courses themselves. Also, it was the perception of both instructors that the pupils did experience psychological growth in the class. They asked more complex questions with greater insight to self and others as the course developed. Also, there were signs of increased group support, namely, students volunteering to help their classmates practice some of the teaching skills. These "atmosphere" changes were also documented through some survey check lists as measures of classroom climate from the Borton-Newberg project (Philadelphia Affective Education Program).

Thus, from a variety of perspectives, the one-term class in cross-age teaching demonstrated a positive impact upon the level of psychological and ethical maturation of the participants. In this way, the results are similar to so-called DPE classes, in which teenagers were involved in a balance between experience and reflection, involved in genuine role taking, around significant interpersonal learning. These include previously reported studies in counseling (Rustad and Rogers),[23] women's development (Erickson),[24] cross-age teaching of moral dilemmas (Mosher and Sullivan)[25] and contemporaneous studies by (Exum, in press) college-age tutoring,[26] and by Glassberg in working with undergraduate pre-service teachers.[27]

From a theoretical standpoint, the major elements of the current program for high school students which seem to account for or explain why it works derive from a series of connected concepts. The content of the experience is both real and significant. The role-taking is genuine and more than the traditional role-playing. The pupils learn the real and complex skills of instructing another person. They are obviously working with real live human beings in an important interpersonal relationship. When compared to some of the so-called "Action Learning" projects currently in vogue, the difference is obvious. Working at the local carwash, a hamburger stand, stuffing envelopes for a political campaign, or a variety of low level (somewhat menial) experiences is simply qualitatively different than the responsible role-taking involved in child care, counseling, or teaching. Romantic vocational and career educationists may think otherwise, but learning experiences are not equally significant. Experience by itself, as Dewey noted, can be educative *or* mis-educative. Recently, Rest provided a careful critique of DPE programs, which he summarized somewhat facetiously by asking (rhetorically) if the requisite for DPE is experience and reflection, then a football game with its huddle and action could qualify as a developmental education.[28] A long answer to this can be found in a recent response. A short answer is that "push-pin is not the same as poetry," teaching a blind child to swim is not the same as working at the Rub-a-Dub-Dub Car Wash.

Thus, one element is the *quality* of the experience, plus the *active* role-taking. The students are not passive observers (or movie-goers in Walker Percy's term).

A second element is that the programs create *dissonance*. Developmental theory assumes that growth and development is not linear nor additive. In other words, we don't simply add-on new experiences and new systems to process meaning. Instead, growth involves a disequilibrium. We have to give up some of the old system to operate at a higher more complex level. New learning, since it requires a cognitive structural change, occurs only through such a process. This creates dissonance since it is by definition upsetting to think and process in new forms.

Cognetta and Sprinthall

Generally, humans at any stage will seek to re-establish and cling to the old, battle change and (at least in part) remain with the familiar and comfortable. Sometimes the growth process is referred to as "jamming." This may be too strong a phrase, but it does describe a central educational feature of developmental programs; namely, that the experience and the classroom discussions "stretch" (in old fashioned terms) the students. Simultaneously, while the pupils are being encouraged and stimulated to think and act at a more complex level, they are also being "supported" in a psychological sense. Their concerns, fears and worries are processed and supported by the instructors *and* they are still asked to do the new activity. For example, the fear that the high schoolers experienced prior to their first teaching experience with the 6th and 7th graders was most evident. The instructors spent a substantial amount of time acknowledging and exploring these fears and said in essence: "We hear your concerns, they are real and genuine - - it's O.K. to feel that way - - and now we're going to help you prepare for your first teaching assignment." We found particularly with adolescents (even more so than with elementary or college age students) that the personal worries and the fear of risking was high not only in the teaching course but in all of the classes we've taught at the high school level, including counseling and child care courses. As noted earlier, Elkind's theory and our own observations suggest that adolescent egocentrism seems to resist and fear the new role-taking and responsibility involved in the more complex functions of these classes. Practically all the students commented on the difficulties in taking such risks, even though afterwards they experienced the positive feelings that accompany doing something well for the first time. At least we view this a requisite for developmental growth: a challenge within the grasp of the students, and the support necessary to "get them over the hump."

SUMMARY

The high school program in cross-age teaching was designed to stimulate aspects of development on the part of the senior high tutors. The curriculum experiences involved a series of structured role-taking opportunities, plus time each week for reflection, reading, discussion and practice. Real experience generally preceded or was concurrent with so-called academic input and content. The results indicated small yet significant increases in the students' level of psychological and ethical maturity. These results were also consistent with other recent or current studies employing similar formats.

The major applied implication of the current study is that such programs are entirely within the reach of most schools. If schools continue to adopt cross-age and peer teaching without a commitment to systematic training/education on the part of the tutors, then a major educational opportunity will be missed. On the other hand, if school personnel (teachers and counselors) are willing to provide regular seminars each week for practice, discussion and readings, then the evidence suggests that the tutors enjoy significant psychological/ethical gains. The seminar provides the environment for experience-based learning to "take." Unexamined experiences (apologies to Socrates), or role-taking without reflection, essentially is equivalent to random education. Intuitively, some may benefit yet others, and probably by far the majority, may remain unaffected by the experience. As noted in the opening essay on Dewey, significant experience requires connectedness and reflection. Cross-age teaching programs employing formats similar to those presented in this and Enright's article can yield benefits in a generic sense to the pupils involved. As educators, should we strive for less?

NOTES and REFERENCES

1. Allen, V. L. (Ed.), *Children as Teachers: Theory and Research on Tutoring.* (New York: Academic Press, 1976).

2. Paolitto, D. P., "The Effects of Cross-age Tutoring on Adolescence: An Inquiry into Theoretical Assumptions," in *Review of Educational Research* (Spring, Vol. 46 (2), 1976), pp. 215-237.

3. Bloom, S., *Peer and Cross-Age Tutoring in the Schools: An Individualized Supplement to Group Instruction.* (Chicago: Chicago Board of Education, District 10, 1975).

4. Allen, *op. cit.,* p. 362.

5. Tyler, R., "Foreword," in A. Gartner, M. C. Kohlber, and F. Riessman, *Children Teach Children: Learning by Teaching,* (New York: Harper and Row, 1971).

6. Coleman, J., et. al., *Youth: Transition to Adulthood: Report of the Panel on Youth.* (Chicago: University of Chicago Press, 1974).

7. Allen, *op. cit.*

8. *Ibid.*

9. Kohlberg, L. and R. Mayer, "Development as the Aim of Education," in *Harvard Educational Review* (42, 4, 1972) pp. 449-496.

10. Gartner, A., M. C. Kohlber, and F. Riessman, *Children Teach Children: Learning by Teaching.* (New York: Harper and Row, 1971).

11. Atkins, V. S., *High School Students Who Teach: An Approach to Personal Learning.* (Unpublished doctoral dissertation, Harvard University Graduate School of Education, 1972).

12. Powell, B. S., *Children As Teachers.* (Unpublished doctoral dissertation, Harvard Graduate School of Education, 1970).

13. Flanders, N. A., *Analyzing Teaching Behavior.* (Reading: Addison-Wesley, 1970).

14. Allen, D. and K. Ryan, *Microteaching.* (Reading: Addison-Wesley, 1969).

15. Gordon, T., *Teacher Effectiveness Training.* (New York: Wyden, 1974).

16. Joyce, B. and M. Weil, *Models of Teaching .* (New Jersey: Prentice Hall, 1972).

17. Elkind, D., *Children and Adolescents.* (New York: Oxford University Press, 1970).

18. Mosher, R. and N. A. Sprinthall, "Deliberate Psychological Education," in *The Counseling Psychologist* (2, 1972) pp. 3-82.

19. Loevinger, J. and R. Wessler, *Measuring Ego Development,* Vols. 1 and 2. (San Francisco: Jossey-Bass, 1970).

20. Elkind, *op. cit.*

21. Gollub, W., *Affective Education Development Program Research Report.* (Philadelphia: Philadelphia School District, 1971).

22. Rest, J. R., *Manual for the Defining Issues Test.* (Minneapolis: University of Minnesota, 1974).

23. Rustad, K. and C. Rogers, "Promoting Psychological Growth in a High School Class," in *Counselor Education and Supervision* (14, 4, 1975), pp. 227-285.

24. Erickson, V. L., "Psychological Growth for Women," in *Counseling and Values* (18, 2, 1974), pp. 102-116.

25. Mosher, R. L. and P. Sullivan, "A Curriculum in Moral Education for Adolescents," in *The Journal of Moral Education* (5, 2, 1976), pp. 159-172.

26. Exum, H. A., *Cross-Age and Peer Teaching.* (Unpublished doctoral dissertation, University of Minnesota, 1977).

27. Glassberg, S., *Peer Supervision for Student Teachers.* (Unpublished doctoral dissertation, University of Minnesota, 1977).

28. Rest, J., "Comments on the Deliberate Psychological Education Programs," in *The Counseling Psychologist* (6, 4, 1977), pp. 32-34.

A Democratic High School: Damn It, Your Feet are Always in the Water

Ralph L. Mosher

> "(Non-democratic government) is like a splendid ship, with all its sails set; it moves majestically on, then it hits a rock and sinks forever. Democracy is like a raft. It never sinks, but damn it, your feet are always in the water."
>
> (D. W. Brogan)

INTRODUCTION

For the past two years, I have been involved as a consultant in an experiment in student self-government of a small alternative high school in Brookline, Massachusetts. This article is an account, essentially impressionistic, of the funny things that happen on the way to school democracy, or what Kohlberg talks about as Stage 5. I think, also, that we now have enough experience to say some considered, tempered things about democracy in school: e.g., that like every constructive, substantial school reform, democratic governance is very hard to vitalize and sustain; or that translating powerful political, educational and psychological theory about democracy into human or institutional behavior and commitments is hard, often frustrating work. I suppose the founding fathers might very well reply: Did anyone ever promise it would be otherwise? All of us underestimate the task it is to mobilize people on behalf of higher ideals. But that it is important to do so, I continue to believe on both ideological and evidentiary grounds.

This account of school democracy is presented in three

parts. The *first* section deals with the origins of our applied research and the critical issue of the definition or meaning of school democracy. Kohlberg's conception of the "just community" school and, in particular, John Dewey's ideas on democracy in education are examined carefully as definitional sources. The *second* section of the paper is a detailed Case Study of the experience of one alternative school in its efforts to become democratic. The purpose is to give a concrete description of what happened in establishing the conditions for, and the process of genuine student self-governance and decision making relative to the school. The *third* section draws more general conclusions regarding school democracy, in terms of both its promises and paradoxes, from our experience to date. Our applied study of school democracy, which is still in progress, continues to be rich in meaning.

Part I, SCHOOL DEMOCRACY: ROOTS

Let me begin with some of the intoxicating and persuasive rhetoric which has moved us to study ways to have high school students learn about democracy directly by governing themselves. Importantly, democracy in a school means more than self-government. Robert Hutchins, in an article entitled "Is Democracy Possible?" contributed to the impetus when he wrote that:

> "Democracy is a system of government by which people rule and are ruled in turn for the good life of the whole. It is a system of self-government by the consent of the governed, who have consented among other things, to majority rule . . . The aim of any democracy must be the common good, which is that good which no member of the community would enjoy if he did not belong to the community. . . The people of the United States are in fact defaulted citizens, with an indifference and even a hostility to government, politics and law that would have astounded . . . the founding fathers. Instead of being

Ralph L. Mosher

a citizen the American individual is a consumer, an object of propaganda and a statistical unit. In view of the condition of our education, our mass media and our political parties the outlook for democracy, the free society and the political community seems dim . . . The founding fathers meant us to learn . . . how to form a more perfect union, to establish justice, to insure domestic tranquility, to provide for the common defense, to promote the general welfare and to secure the blessings of liberty to ourselves and our posterity. They founded a political community; a community learning together to discover and achieve the common good, the elements of which they set forth, but did not elucidate, in the Preamble . . . The Constitution is to be interpreted, therefore, as a charter of learning. We are to learn how to develop the seeds the fathers planted under the conditions of our own time . . . What would be unconstitutional would be limitations or inhibitions on learning. Today freedom and justice demand that equality be applied to opportunities for each citizen to achieve his fullest possible development. This means equal educational opportunity. It also means access to the legal system, to the health system, to housing. The political community cannot be restored or maintained unless minorities and the poor are given that equality to which this community was originally dedicated . . . We must revive, reconstruct and learn to operate the political community in the United States because the task we confront on our 200th anniversary is nothing less than the organization of the world political community."[1]

The gap between the latter vision and my modest effort to assist one school to become democratic is sobering. Nonetheless, Hutchins' imperatives make the case for learning democracy unequivocal. They cut like a January wind in New England to the political, constitutional and moral (i.e., the American) case for vitalizing in each generation, the "truths in which America was conceived." Powerful ideas, after all, are the only ones worth holding to.

The Democratic School as a Means to Stimulate Students' Moral Development:

A second impetus to my study of democracy in school has been Lawrence Kohlberg's research on moral development and moral education. Kohlberg is best known for a theory of moral development describing how our thinking concerning right and wrong evolves, what we ought to do, questions of value, and what our rights and obligations are. He has found that our moral reasoning becomes both intellectually more complex and morally more principled - i.e., that it "develops." There are, in this process, identifiable stages or characteristic ways of thinking morally; experience, not the calendar, causes this evolution to occur. One whole stage of moral reasoning in Kohlberg's theory, Stage 5, describes the moral ideology underlying the Constitution and the democratic process. These self evident truths are that all people are created equal, that they have certain inalienable rights: to be free, to own property, to achieve their fullest possible development; that people create community to secure these rights and to effect the greatest good for the greatest number of citizens; that they make and apply fair laws protecting these rights to all; that government is accountable to the people; that every citizen has an equal vote, voice and obligation in the definition and management of the community. (In passing, it merits mentioning how critical a term "mutual obligation" is to the hard, frustrating work of sustaining the *polis.)*

Significantly, Kohlberg's data suggest that Stage 5 moral reasoning is used by only 20 percent of adult Americans and by few adolescents, although it can be understood, intuitively, by a larger proportion of people. If true, this may explain why the Equal Rights Amendment has yet to pass, why equality of opportunity or access to education, justice, medical care and jobs is denied to so many people; why democracy is so hard to establish and sustain; why the American

Ralph L. Mosher

revolution is unfinished. Kohlberg sees the problem partly in psychological terms - i.e., that the moral and rational capacity for full democracy and justice is latent in human thought and must be stimulated by experience (i.e., by education and, in particular, through living in a community that is democratic and just). It is clear also that Kohlberg's essential preoccupation (and moral principle) is justice, and that constitutional democracy is *one* procedural means to bring about justice. Kohlberg argues that the central objective of moral education is to promote justice in individuals and in human institutions. To do that requires a community where real moral issues of justice, rights and obligations are decided by all. His own applied research has involved creating and studying such "just" communities in prison and school. The democratic school project reported here is broadly influenced by Kohlberg's psychology. By intention, however, it does not conform to the exact modus operandi, organizational structure or justice ideology of Kohlberg's prison or school studies. Democracy or justice does not have one, Platonic institutional definition or form; it is especially important for people to be democratic according to self-selected general principles, rather than specific practices.

John Dewey: The Philosopher of Democracy

In a philosophical sense, the real roots of my efforts at democratizing schooling lie in the writings of John Dewey. The discussion of Dewey which follows is organized around two objectives. *First,* it is intended to help clarify what I mean by school or classroom democracy. My bias is that it is very difficult to innovate in schools (e.g., to effect "moral education," "school democracy" or a "just community") without clear definitions of what is intended. I do believe that, over time, an alternating cycle of hard *thinking* and carefully examined *practice* helps us understand something like school democracy in its full applied complexity. But definitional clarity is critical to me, and I turned to Dewey for the help. I looked, also, for the most profound definitions and was agreeably surprised in the process.

Second, the aspects of Dewey's thinking relative to school democracy cited here are selected in part because they speak to problems in the realization of this process at the School-Within-A-School. Specifically, our efforts have encountered at least the following hard questions: Is school democracy essentially student self-government? Is that all there is? Can self-government, in fact, be a substantial enough process to affect students? If school democracy is more than self-government, what more? Is is possible for a group of students, relatively homogenous in terms of race, social class, or ethnicity to be democratic? To what extent is the individual in a democratic school free to do his own thing (e.g., to ignore his school community, its rules, its governance, or its development)? What claims may a democratic school fairly make of its members, and what obligations has a student in a democratic school? What purposes and processes uniquely characterize a democratic alternative school? It was with these very thorny and practical issues in the implementation of school democracy in mind that I read Dewey.

Democracy as Self-Government:

In contrast to some of Dewey's other writing, the conceptions of democracy he offered are complex, but not obscure. He talked, first, about democracy as a political process. Most people, I suppose, would so construe it. (Note Hutchins' emphasis on democracy as a system of self-government.)

> "Democracy is a special political form, a method
> of conducting government, of making laws and
> carrying on governmental administration by
> means of popular suffrage and elected officers."[2]

Dewey described political democracy in familiar terms: as a way to effect the will and the interests of the majority of the people where consent is freely given to the purposes and the

Ralph L. Mosher

rules by which the individual or the institution is to live. Agreement as to the common purposes, rights and obligations is embodied in a social contract; the political procedures in a democracy insure the right of the individual to a voice and a vote in its decisions.

The Democratic Way of Life:
Many Shared Interests and An Open Door:

Dewey was quick to stress that these political procedures were *means* for realizing democracy as the truly human *way of living*. Democracy, he argued, is more than a form of government; it is primarily a way of living together. And the democratic community will have two essential characteristics: *the interests its members consciously share will be numerous and varied, and it will have a full and free interaction with other forms of social association.* Thus, a democratic community (whether it be a classroom, school, New England village or a nation-state) will share many common interests which require the individual member to consider the views, wishes and claims of others relative to these common concerns. When the individual identifies and pursues such common interests with others, he will hear, at least, conflicting opinions and claims and may come to consider them against some criterion such as the preferences of his friends, neighborhood interests, the law, majority interest and will, or a principle such as fairness. Taking the perspective of others into account begins to break down the barriers of which obviously are antithetical to viewing individuals as equal in either a constitutional or a moral sense. The greater the diversity of people pursuing common interests, the more encompassing in his viewpoint the individual may come to be.

Dewey, too, was interested in the relationship between the society (or the political process in which the individual lived) and what he learned from it. Thus, he recognized that we learn from novelty and that the greater the diversity of people we encounter, not as tourists but around common objectives, the more we are likely to learn. Nothing is so profoundly educative as to live in another culture. Democracy, ideally, would have us live with different people and cultures (e.g., the Irish Catholics of South Boston, the Jews of Newton) within our broader community but with whom we had to work out tasks in common.

For the same reasons, (i.e., role taking opportunities, the reduction of stereotyping) Dewey argued that a democratic group will be characterized by full and free interactions with other social groups in the community-at-large (e.g., young people, workers, blacks, women, etc.).

> "The two points by which to measure the worth of a form of social life are the extent in which the interests of a group are shared by all its members and the fullness and freeness with which it interacts with other groups. An undesirable society . . . is one which internally and externally sets up barriers to free intercourse and communication of experience. A society which makes provision for participation in its good of all its members on equal terms and which secures flexible re-adjustment of its institutions through interaction of the different forms of associated life is in so far democratic."[3]

Two contemporary educators, Newmann and Oliver, have argued that:

> ". . the most fundamental objective of education is the development of individual human dignity or self realization within community. The broadly stated objective can be specified in many ways, emphasizing either individualism or social association. However one defines dignity or fulfillment, the nature of the society within which it develops is critical . . . Every educator . . . should be able, therefore, to explicate and clarify the particular conception of society or community upon which he justifies educational recommendations."[4]

Ralph L. Mosher

For Dewey the answer is clear: democracy, with the characteristics identified above, is an ideal form of social association
and, as well, an ideal education for self-realization. The question of the evidence for this remarkable claim is an interesting
one. Dewey simply said it was so and, then, offered moral
and psychological arguments in support. Scharf points to the
lineage of support for this claim:

> "It has long been established that participation in dem-
> ocratically organized institutions is associated with
> rapid social development. Both Cooley (1916) and
> Mead (1933) suggested that democratic groups offer
> possibilities for interdependence and mutual sharing
> not found in authoritarian groups. Lewin (1954) sug-
> gests likewise that ideological change occurs more
> rapidly in democratic groups allowing for a shared
> sense of control and for opportunities for dissent."[5]

For Dewey, the individual and society are inextricable. The
process of the individual's development is an enlargement of
his social perspective and his social and moral commitments -
a fundamental progression empirically validated by all contemporary psychological theories of development (e.g., Piaget,
Kohlberg, Loevinger). Kateb has argued the same point:

> ". . the process of self-realization is a process of
> continuous involvement with society."[6]

Dewey's more quaint and prior statement was that:

> "The cause of education . . . is one of development,
> focusing indeed in the growth of students, but to
> be conceived even in this connection as part of
> the larger development of society."[7]

Individual Freedom in a Democracy:

Dewey was concerned that democracy, with its belief in
legal and constitutional equality and the maximizing of individual liberty can be understood as unbridled individualism:

a hunting license and a twelve month open season for "doing one's own thing." Tocqueville, much earlier, had remarked that democracy fosters individualism and that individualism first saps the virtues of public life and ends in pure selfishness. Americans would be forced, he predicted, by the necessity of cooperating in the management of their free institutions and by their desire to exercise political rights, into the habit of attending to the interests of the public. Unfettered freedom to be oneself and to do one's thing continues to have much appeal, however. And that is true not only for radical educators, with their passionate desire to liberate mankind from culture with its patterns and authority, but also for faculty or students in the alternative high school in question, who do not see community as prior to the individual. But Dewey was clear that democracy is an interaction between society and selves:

> " The democratic idea of freedom is not the right of
> each individual to *do* as he pleases, even if it be
> qualified by adding 'provided he does not interfere
> with the same freedom on the part of others' . . .the
> basic freedom is that of freedom of *mind* and of
> whatever degree of freedom of action and experience
> is necessary to produce freedom of intelligence. The
> modes of freedom guaranteed in the Bill of Rights are
> all of this nature: Freedom of belief and conscience,
> of expression of opinion, of assembly for discussion
> and conference, of the press as an organ of commu-
> nication. They are guaranteed because without them
> individuals are not free to develop and society is
> deprived of what they might contribute."[8]

Democracy as an Acquired Taste:

Dewey also knew that democracy, unlike the wheel, must be continually re-discovered in people's understanding and in the institutions they create. It is an idea and a process which, by definition, has to be "re-invented" through the hard

Ralph L. Mosher

thinking, practice and majority consent of each group of people trying to be democratic. Thus, a democratic school will be what its *members* decide is a democratic school. It is interesting to note the parallels in Dewey's thinking to Hutchins' observations, cited earlier, that "The Constitution is to be interpreted, therefore, as a charter of learning."

Dewey argued further that the re-invention of democracy in the individual's understanding and in our institutions must go beyond knowledge or information about "the anatomy of the government" (studying the federal and state constitutions, the names and duties of all of the officers, etc.) to *understanding* "the things that are done, that need to be done and how to do them."[9] Here he is saying that people need an understanding of democracy that permits them to *be* democratic.

> "If the classes in our schools asked, 'What would
> have to be done to give us genuine democratic
> government in our states, local communities and
> nation?' I think it is certainly true that a great
> many things had to be looked into and a great
> deal more knowledge obtained than is acquired
> as long as we simply take our democratic govern-
> ment as a fact and don't ask either how it is
> actively run or how it might be run."[10]

Elsewhere Dewey says:

> "Schools in a democracy . . . must be willing to
> undertake whatever re-organization of studies,
> of methods of teaching, of administration inclu-
> ding that larger organization which concerns
> the relation of pupils and teachers to each other
> and to the life of the community."[11]

From this it seems evident that Dewey was prepared to go whatever distance was necessary to educate people both to understand democracy and to be democratic.

Given his recognition of the profoundly educative effect

of the social groups and institutions in which the individual participates, it is not surprising that Dewey argued that democracy cannot be taught or understood in institutions (e.g., schools or families) which are non-democratic. Neither old fashioned civics classes, newer political science methodologies and theories (e.g., systems analysis, a la Gillespie and Patrick),[12] nor student government can do more than caricature democracy in repressive institutions, such as that portrayed in Fredrick Wiseman's documentary, **High School**. As Dewey said, so pointedly:

> "Whether the education process is carried on in a
> predominantly democratic or non-democratic
> way becomes, therefore, a question of transcen-
> dent importance not only for education itself
> but for its final effect upon all the interests and
> activities of a society that is committed to the
> democratic way of life."[13]

The point is that, if we are serious about educating for democracy, we will have to begin to democratize classroom management, school governance, the relations between administrators, teachers and students; a task whose complexity may be exceeded only by its enduring significance. Of the practical complexities of this task, more shortly.

Elements in the Democratic Creed:

Dewey talked about two articles of faith which are fundamental for any democrat or democratic educator. They are also notably American in their optimism and confidence in the further progress or evolution of human personality. These are that democracy requires a basic commitment to the reasonableness, the potential fairness of, as well as the human frailties of, each group trying to be democratic.

> "A faith in the capacities of human nature; faith
> in human intelligence and in the power of pooled

Ralph L. Mosher

and cooperative experience. It is not belief that
these things are complete but that if given a show,
they will grow and be able to generate progres-
sively the knowledge and wisdom needed to guide
collective action."[14]

Second, is a belief in the equality of human beings. Dewey is careful to point out that this is not a belief that all people are psychologically equal (e.g., in terms of intelligence, judgment or character). Rather, they are legally, constitutionally and morally equal. As individuals, they are, as a matter of fact, markedly different in capacity and achievement but, in terms of their rights/claims, they are equal. Their legal and consti-tutional rights are foundational and uncompromisable in a democratic society, as is *the opportunity of every indivi-dual to develop to his full capacity.*[15] It is significant that Hutchins, in analyzing the unfinished American revolution a generation later, makes the same point. "Today freedom and justice demand that equality be applied to opportunities for each citizen to achieve his fullest possible development."

Good Fences Do Not Make Good Democrats:

Dewey made at least one other observation about dem-ocracy which is important for educators. It is, that any of us deprived, for whatever reasons, of significant interaction with classes or groups of people different than ourselves (e.g., Blacks, Chicanos, Jews, Evangelical Christians, homo-sexuals, Florida orange growers, even Anita Bryant) are denied significant opportunities for growth in our understanding of that separation. The privileged who live in $150,000 homes in the planned, idyllic, amenity-rich communities of southern California are deprived in the same way that their Chicano gardeners are deprived: of learning that talent, intelligence, character, strength (as well as frailty) exists in all of us and is at least as common and characteristic as is our blackness, our Jewishness, our Protestant ethic. Stated more pretentiously, it is precisely these experiences of strangers which help us to see our common aspirations, goodness and humanity and the essential respect which all of us, as individuals, deserve. In this sense, Dewey was saying that good fences do not make good neighbors, that unfamiliarity, not familiarity, breeds and sustains contempt between people.

Democracy - The Governance, Social and Education Conditions to Stimulate All-around Student Growth:

Dewey's most encompassing definition of school democracy is stated indelibly in the following excerpt: *"All social institutions have a meaning, a purpose. That purpose is to set free and to develop the capacities of human individuals, without respect to race, sex, class or economic status . . . The test of their value is the extent to which they educate every individual into the full stature of his possibility. Democracy has many meanings, but if it has a moral meaning, it is found in resolving that the supreme test of all political institutions and industrial arrangements shall be the contribution they make to the all-around growth of every member of society."*[16]
I risk being gratuitous to stress that Dewey was saying schools are democratic in the extent to which they contribute to the all-around growth of every student. In another paper in this issue, Sprinthall and I have discussed Dewey's correlative and fundamental belief that the aim of education is the development of individuals to the utmost of their potentialities. In arguing for the democratic *administration* of schools, he says: "All schools that pride themselves upon being up-to-date utilize methods of instruction that draw upon and utilize the life-experience of students and strive to individualize the treatment of pupils. Whatever reasons hold for adopting this course with respect to the young certainly more strongly hold for teachers, since the latter are more mature and have more experience."[17] We have reviewed in this article what Dewey said about teaching students "understanding" of how to do and be democratic; his arguments

that democracy is an ideal form for human relationships and a way of living together optimal for the development of human personality, and the diminishing effects on all groups of the exclusion of any "have not" group from full participation and their legal/moral rights in a democracy. The conclusion is inescapable . . . Dewey meant to create in schools the governance, social and curricular-instructional conditions supportive of childrens' full development. That is the ultimate criterion of a fully democratic school.

Presumably Dewey recognized, although he did not say, that children would be at very different points in their understanding and skill in democracy, just as their schools could be at very different stages of becoming democratic. One of the things we are learning from our present studies of the effects of democracy on children is the converse: i.e., how dependent students' understanding of democracy is on the stage of their cognitive, moral and personal-social development. Students at Kohlberg's Stages 2 or 3 understand and appropriate the experience of democracy in their school very differently from students at Stages 4, 4½ or 5. Further, it appears that schools or groups of teachers, students and administrators trying to be democratic will collectively understand and represent democracy in qualitatively different ways, and that we should expect this to be so.

The evolution of democratic schools *from* titular student government (the present norm) *to* self-governance *to* communities offering equality of access to the social, governance and educative conditions for every individual to develop to his full capacity presumably will take as long to realize as it will in the larger American community. How long that may take has been documented by Lispset and Schneider in an article entitled "America's Schizophrenia on Achieving Equality."[18] But it is important to recognize as Dewey did (and for which modern developmental psychology can offer certain plausible explanations) that this progression will not happen in a day, a year, or a decade; that it will occur in individuals or institutions in stages, and that Stage 2 and Stage 3 democratic schools (and students) have integrity, just as certainly as a caterpillar, a cocoon and a butterfly are representations of one evolving organism. Of this, more later.

To conclude this section on the critical task of defining school democracy, it is evident, I feel, that much of what one needs to know about democracy and education is there in broad conception in Dewey's writings. I also suspect that teachers, administrators, students and parents, in trying to democratize their school, or parts of it, will have to rediscover, through such experience, what Dewey, Kohlberg or I may have learned. I think that would hearten rather than surprise any of us. As Dewey said, writing forty years ago:

> "I can think of nothing so important in this country
> at present as a rethinking of democracy and its im-
> plications. Neither the rethinking nor the action it
> should produce can be brought into being in a day
> or a year: The democratic idea itself demands that
> the thinking and the activity proceed cooperatively.
> My utmost hope will be fulfilled if anything I have
> said plays any part, however small, in promoting co-
> operative inquiry and experimentation in this field
> of the democratic administration of our schools."[19]

Part II, THE SCHOOL-WITHIN-A-SCHOOL: AN ON-GOING CASE STUDY OF STUDENT SELF-GOVERNMENT

The School-Within-A-School (S.W.S.), an alternative school which is part of Brookline High School in Brookline, Massachusetts, was established in 1969. Its roots were in the turbulence and unrest then affecting the nation's institutions of higher education, as well as many secondary schools. A group of students, teachers and parents proposed to the school committee an alternative school which would offer the students a larger voice in their education and a more equal and

Ralph L. Mosher

personal relationship with teachers. One of the enduring emphases from that period is what appears genuinely to be a more equal and personal relationship between the students and teachers. Students are intimately known to the staff and treated with respect as individuals—key elements in the earlier definitions of a democratic group. Certainly the present enrichment curriculum gives students the opportunity to *learn* and *do* many things. If one understanding of the ultimate democratic school is as a community offering the social, governance and educative conditions supportive of the full development of every student in it, then the enrichment courses are an important *means* - just as is the school's process of self-governance - to that end. How well any means works, in particular, how much it is part of a conscious and coherent effort to be a democratic school - is less clear in the case of S.W.S.

Another legacy of the school's origin may be the remarkable freedom which students have in their celebration and casualness and, at times, their abuse of it. In any event, S.W.S. students would feel much at home with the ideology of New Hampshire's license plates: "Live free or die." One of the critical (and classical) issues in this school is the extent to which the community - in terms of shared purposes - can be established/constructed in relation to freedom for the individual student. Dewey's point that:

> "The system of liberties that exists at any time is
> always the system of restraints or controls that
> exists at that time. No one can *do* anything except
> in relation to what others can do and cannot do."[20]

has yet to be understood in S.W.S. John Locke's observation that:

> ". . . one of our essential freedoms is the freedom to
> have obligations and that those who fail to under-
> stand this are doomed to perpetual immaturity."[21]

is a related point of view whose time has yet to come for some students at S.W.S. Of this, more later.

In the Beginning

When I first became involved with S.W.S. in the spring of 1975, school rules and policy were made largely by the director and staff. Students were encouraged to attend staff meetings at which rules and policies were discussed, and to voice their views. Sharp or angry conflicts between students and staff were rare or absent, but there was some concern - on the part of the staff and a proportion of the students - that S.W.S. did not have enough sense of purpose and community. The general lack of community, uneasiness about a small unrepresentative governing body and an interest in the Danforth Moral Education Project, then ongoing in Brookline, influenced the staff and some interested students to pursue the "just community" approach. An initial ballot vote established clear support for developing democratic self-governance procedures.

This point may be of some small historical interest. Of all the present generation "just community" school projects - in Cambridge, Pittsburgh, California and elsewhere, the S.W.S. students - not a group of parents, teachers or consultants - voted for democracy as self-government of their school. In the subsequent, rocky evolution of the project that fact has made, it seems, little qualitative difference in their degree of commitment to school democracy. It is in the nature of many adolescents (and academics) I have known to be better at talking than doing, to forget commitments, to be tentative or irresponsible. But as consultants we did not come to these modern day Thoreaus with the conscious design of doing them good, nor did they run for their lives. Our position was that we would assist them in their efforts to establish self-governance and would remain as long as that was a central commitment, or until asked to leave. The former coordinator, Diane Ryan, put it succinctly: "We didn't buy a moral education package, but we are applying the principles in our decision making. It's a very good marriage."[22]

A brief description of S.W.S. is in order. It is a part of

Ralph L. Mosher

Brookline High School - occupying three classrooms (instant Goodwill Enterprises in decor) and an office. It can accommodate an enrollment of up to 100 students, having that number enrolled at the time of writing. There is now a waiting list for admission (the first time that has been the case). The staff includes two half-time English teachers, one full-time math and science teacher, a half-time social studies teacher and a full-time coordinator and counselor. Most students take at least two courses in S.W.S. (a policy voted by the school in its first year of democratic self-governance - largely to protect the positions of the teachers), and the rest of their academic load in the regular high school. The S.W.S. classes themselves are traditional in content; the difference is mainly in the classroom atmosphere - which is relaxed - and in the students' relationships with teachers, which, as noted, are more personal. "S.W.S. is an 'alternative' to a traditional setting in terms of the way the school is run more than in terms of the content of the curriculum."[23] The enrichment program, as noted, is an added feature of the curriculum. Its classes are usually held in the evening and students, teachers, parents and others - such as university professors like me - may offer courses. The goals for students are stated as:

1) taking as much responsibility for their own education as possible;

2) sharing in the governance of S.W.S.;

3) contributing to the building of the S.W.S. community.[24]

The basic assumptions with which our consultation at S.W.S. began were several. It is important to stress the word "began." These glib declarative sentences from the Danforth proposal have been altered by what we have learned since.

"a) Programs in moral education must go beyond the classroom discussion of moral dilemmas to effect, directly, the justice structure of the school (i.e., its rules and discipline, the process by which they are decided, the rights and responsibilities of the students and staff, etc.).

b) Students, given instruction and support, can govern themselves. In so doing, they experience the complexity of real moral decision and choice and see the consequences of such decisions both for individual students and their school as a community.

c) In the process of governing their own school, students learn important democratic or parliamentary skills (e.g., how to chair a meeting, how to establish an agenda, how to speak to the point). They also learn to take into account the perspective and rights of other students and staff and will develop more comprehensive and fairer thinking. In a broader sense, the present studies of the democratic school are concerned not only to teach students essential democratic and citizen participation knowledge and skills, they further assume that such systematic experience will have significant developmental effect on the students' social growth and moral reasoning."[25]

Fortunately, our study of the relationship betweeen democracy as a process and how people are affected by it also began with the demurrer that we were "in an early phase of educational development and testing" and with a number of questions:

"How best to begin democratic governance experiments in different high schools; what are the practical organizational units of the high school (e.g., individual classrooms, alternative schools, houses?) in which to introduce student self-government; how to vitalize representative student government; how to develop formal courses (e.g., in social studies, law, English) which inform, analyze and support experience in student self-government; how to educate students, teachers, administrators, parents to make school democracy workable; the appropriateness of such experiences for students at junior high school and middle school level, etc. are examples of the questions concerning which much further educational development remains to be done."[26]

Again, and in retrospect, it is interesting to note the re-iterative equation of student self-government and school democracy in the excerpts. That is simply a reflection of the fact that I had not done my homework on democracy in education. Despite the demurrers, I underestimated the degree to which democracy is a very complex ideal, idea and process either to understand or to make real in a school. I was to learn much more about democracy from S.W.S. than I would be able to contribute at first. This paper, among other things, is part of an ongoing effort to do that homework, to create knowledge from practice and to balance my indebtedness to S.W.S. But it is especially sobering to realize how many of the questions we have identified remain to be answered.

Two Years Before the Mast

In this section I will summarize the main developments over the two years of our association with S.W.S. I will not do so in the detail necessary for the reader to go and do likewise. As noted before, democracy is a process which, by definition, has to be "re-invented" by people trying to *be* democratic. Any idea papers or descriptions of just or democratic schools should be understood against this prior qualification (i.e., S.W.S. as a democratic school ultimately will be what its *members* decide is a democratic school). Impressive participant observation and empirical studies of just high schools or democratic classes are already available.[27] Finally, the structure of meaning we make of this experience at S.W.S. is more pertinent than its concrete details. Hopefully, what follows will summarize adequately some of the funny things that have happened on the way to Stage 5 (see also Section III).

Year 1:

In September of 1975, there was an air of curiosity and excitement about the impending changes in the governance structure of S.W.S. Initially, the students became quite involved in elaborate discussions about the structure of the weekly community meetings. Much debate was given to establishing fair procedures, such as developing rules of order for the community meetings, determining a way to set agenda, and choosing a chairperson. The students and staff were ready to discuss whether the town meetings, as they came to be called (perhaps not surprising in New England), should be mandatory. This issue continued to be raised throughout the first two years of the participatory democracy. In many respects it has embodied the tension in shifting from the school's tradition of autonomy for the individual toward a democratic community. The classic dilemma, of course, is the individual's freedom "to do his thing" in relation (not versus) to the need to work together to achieve common purposes, to build a school where kids know teachers and one another, care about others, are fair to one another, govern themselves - in which every one has a full chance to develop his special talents and interests, etc. Changes in the students' thinking and the impact of the new governance structure may have been reflected in a gradual shift from a position of maximum freedom for the individual student toward an increasing recognition that S.W.S. - as their social community and school - was the responsibility of every student. Certainly, this recurrent issue generated heated debate throughout the first year, but mandatory town meetings were defeated on each of several formal votes, although by increasingly small margins. (It was not until the end of the following year that mandatory town meetings were to be voted by the students).

The consultants (Professor Peter Scharf, Nancy Richardson, Dr. Diana Paolitto, and the author) encouraged the staff to turn over as many issues as possible to the town meeting. Gradually, the staff helped students to share decision-making in such genuinely sensitive issues as attendance policies (what to do with truants or the chronic absenteeism from home rooms), discipline, admissions procedures and the curriculum. The discussions which occurred during the town meetings were quite sophisticated, often centering on abstract issues. At first, the students were more comfortable with such issues and were reluctant to discuss individuals or to make judgments about their peers. For example, the students, in a discussion of "the violation of another person's rights," were reticent about discussing S.W.S. students who were smoking, and acting disrespectfully to teachers in the quadrangle outside the school. However, when a student brought up an incident involving the restriction - by the School Administration - of a group of S.W.S. students' right to freedom of speech, the community became actively engaged. Discussions about the limits of freedom of speech, the meaning of words such as "facts" and "slanderous," and the issue of responsible reporting were the focus of a number of community meetings. These culminated in a well-thought-out letter which was sent to the editor of the school newspaper and to the principal of the larger high school. As a result, the Headmaster agreed to form a committee to establish the specific criteria which should be used for determining whether or not a poster should be displayed in the high school.

A number of other interesting discussions occurred around the criteria for selecting students for S.W.S., the question of whether students who were enrolled in the larger high school should be allowed to take courses at S.W.S., and the process to be used for selecting new staff members. Again, there was a slowly emerging tendency to create policies which recognized the need to restrict certain individual choices in order to legitimize and maximize the growth of the community. These included a rule which required that a student take at least two courses for credit in S.W.S. and the creating of an AWOL (absent without leave) committee, which placed restrictions on the number of times a person could skip a class. The AWOL committee met with students who were missing school in order to determine whether there were problems which might be resolvable with the help of the community.

The Consultants' Role:

A brief mention of the role of the consultants to S.W.S. in Year 1 is in order: Nancy Richardson took primary responsibility for the town meetings. She met each week with members of the Agenda Committee to establish the topic for Town Meeting and to outline the justice/moral issues in connection with these topics. She also spent time with the students who chaired the meetings to teach them leadership skills and rules of order adapted from Parliamentary procedure. She and Peter Scharf met regularly with the staff to discuss the progress of the school and to help them share their authority and power effectively with the students as a whole. She also served during Town Meetings as a "friend of the chair" (really as a Speaker to whom complicated procedural questions were appealed).

Professor Scharf was more directly involved with staff development. S.W.S. teachers expressed concern about wanting their classes to reflect the just community philosophy. They wanted to learn how to teach their classes more democratically and how to apply developmental psychology to their curriculum planning and presentation. During Town Meetings, he acted as a catalyst for examining the issues being discussed from as many different perspectives as possible. This function often involved introducing a conflicting viewpoint or asking students to be explicit about the assumptions underlying their reasoning. My own role in Year 1 was that of a harried participant-observer. To learn about democracy requires an

Ralph L. Mosher

investment of both hard thinking and hard practice: I really did too little of either.

Overall, it is probably reasonable to characterize "the first year of the S.W.S. community (as) largely a year of establishing, legitimizing and refining a new governance structure which allows and requires that all major issues affecting the community be debated and resolved in the Town Meeting. The community is clearly pleased with and committed to the governance structure . . . It voted, without dissent, continuation of the new town meeting form of government and the Danforth consultants for 1976-77. The intention is that the second year will be a year of developing more fully the skills which are required to maintain this structure. Also, there is general interest in conducting a systematic evaluation study which would determine the impact of the just community on the individual student's level of moral reasoning and on the moral climate of the institution."[28]

Year 2:
Snatching Victory from the Jaws of Defeat

A story is told about President Nathan Pusey of Harvard. During the height of the campus turmoil in 1969, he was asked by a friend, "How are things going?" Pusey's reply was: "Well, some days you win and some days you lose. My problem is I can't tell the difference any more." That story is pertinent to an unbiased effort to summarize Year 2 at S.W.S. I think it is safe to say that the democratic school project went through a period of considerable crisis, yet managed to snatch a victory from the jaws of defeat. There were at least three sources of uncertainty in the project.

First, a *mea culpa.* As a new principal consultant to the staff, I was clear neither about the meaning of democracy in a school, nor how to go about its practical implementation at S.W.S. I had bits and pieces of the necessary understanding, but I spent my year going back and forth from **Robert's Rules of Order**[29] to **Democracy and Education** to Kohlberg and

Town Meetings in a cram course. My honest uncertainty limited my ability to assist the staff or the community until late in the year (indeed, it must have made me seem like the Wizard-of-Oz at the moment-of-truth with Dorothy, the Cowardly Lion, the Scarecrow and the Tin Woodman). I draw some comfort from the fact that I was learning much of what I needed to know in the process. Significantly, Fenton reports analogous difficulties in the first operational year at the Civic Education Project in Pittsburgh:

> "The heart of the problem came from inexperience of the entire staff. None of us had run a community meeting; none of us had run an advisory group; none of us had organized a program of community building exercises and only one of us had given a course in interpersonal skills. We made many mistakes as we learned new skills and developed new materials and techniques."[30]

The point is obvious. Where we are attempting change as complex and as unfamiliar in real understanding and practice as democracy is to schools, teachers, students and consultants (even if it is democracy defined as narrowly as self-government), we should expect tough sledding at first.

Second, staff changes in the School-Within-A-School introduced a further source of uncertainty. The former Co-ordinator took a leave of absence, and then resigned. The new Co-ordinator was not confirmed until April. Three part-time teachers will be staff members during 1977-1978. The effect has been to move to a larger and predominantly part-time faculty. Inevitably, commitments must be affected. Further,

> ". . . not all of the staff is in total agreement with the moral education project and therefore not wholly committed . . . There is certainly no hostility or lack of co-operation among the staff nor is there, however, enthusiastic acceptance, which I see as a distinct drawback in the

Ralph L. Mosher

ultimate implementation of the program with
any degree of energy and commitment."[31]

Again, the point is clear. *Without teachers who are committed
to it, school democracy won't happen.* Staff turn-over further
complicates any school innovation, especially in a small alternative high school where the individual teacher has great personal influence.

Third, related to the issue of a part-time staff is the problem of a part-time student body. Many students have only
two classes at S.W.S. and, consequently, are not around a
great deal. Further, a number of students have active lives
and ties in the regular high school, which inevitably dilutes
their commitment to the Town Meeting form of self-government, to S.W.S. and its very vitality as an alternative school.
It is clear that the students' very different understanding of
commitment to, and ability to be democratic, is the most
severe challenge facing this project. As is true of the much
celebrated New England Town Meeting, where the estimate
is that approximately four per cent of the eligible voters
attend, there are many students in S.W.S. who are indifferent
to self-government. This very basic issue will be returned to
in Section III of the paper.

The Business Before the House

Against this backdrop of some of the constraints encountered in establishing school governance at S.W.S., it is important to describe the range and complexity of the issues which
Town Meeting dealt with throughout the year. These have included a policy for student withdrawal from classes; the reporting to Town Meeting of what is discussed in the staff
meetings; a policy for visitors; the need for active recruitment
of new members; S.W.S. policy relative to a new Massachusetts law requiring a moment of silence at the beginning of
each school day; a grading policy for S.W.S.; a probing review
of a research proposal from the Harvard Center for moral

education; the problem of cliques in S.W.S.; how to improve Town Meeting with a revision and relaxing of the rules of order; behavioral guidelines for S.W.S. parties; Black history week and S.W.S. policy toward the racial issues it created; the appointment of two half-time English teachers for 1977-78; the appointment of a new Coordinator; how to stengthen S.W.S. as a community, including the planning of a day-long retreat; the issue of a member's obligations to S.W.S.; the approval of mandatory Town Meetings in 1977-78; the constituting of student advisory groups for the next year, etc. As a regular participant observer, I would characterize discussion of these issues as serious (if sometimes desultory around what were termed "mickey mouse" - i.e., school maintenance issues), protracted (often too much so for the preference of some students) and unquestionably decisive as to official school policy. How well the community remembers or effects commonly decided policy is less clear - certainly enough to get by. Nor, in my judgement, did the community duck or finesse any issue - with the exception of the observance of the moment-of-silence. Students became very competent in chairing Town Meetings - even appointing a student speaker to replace the project consultant in that role. Membership on the Agenda Committee was much sought after; interestingly, in 1977-78 all students will be eligible to serve on the Agenda Committee through a lottery system.

Three other standing Committees continued to function in 1977-78: the Hiring, Waiver and A.W.O.L. Committees. The Hiring Committee, comprised of five students and four staff, was directly involved in the interviewing and appointment of the new part-time English teacher. Decisions regarding the appointment of the other half-time English teacher and the Coordinator's position were made, as noted, by Town Meeting. As one candidate expressed it: "It is far from a rubber stamp group. I was interviewed in September for the intern position - my internship rested on the Committee's decision!" The A.W.O.L. Committee basically deals with students who have been referred to it for cutting classes. Teacher notification of cuts come directly to this Committee rather than to parents. The Committee, meeting with the student, determines the reasons for the student's absences and an appropriate plan.

> "The idea behind this is that students can help
> other students and, as community members,
> have a responsibility to do so; also, ultimately
> students are responsible for their own behavior
> (the reason why parents are not notified)."[32]

In S.W.S. the A.W.O.L. Committee is the only Discipline Committee *per se*, unlike the Cambridge Cluster School, which has a Committee designed to enforce all school rules. Decisions of the Discipline Committee at the Cluster School are often appealed to the community meeting which leads to fruitful discussions regarding fairness. The Waiver Committee is made up of one faculty member, the Coordinator and three students, chosen randomly from volunteers and is concerned primarily with student appeals to drop classes or to schedule classes or working during Town Meeting time. An individual contract is set up with each student waived.

So What is the State of the Union at the End of Year 2?:

Town Meeting met twice weekly. The Standing Committees, too, functioned regularly. In the process, substantial issues were discussed and important policy decisions made. The problem of Town Meeting was not so much the rules of the house, which were modified in response to student and staff criticism - generally in the direction of less formal procedures - nor in the ability of the community to debate or decide, which is really at an impressive level. The problem of Town Meeting was in the unevenness/paucity of the issues brought before it. When the issue was seen as vital (e.g., the reappointment of a favorite teacher), Town Meeting was seen as vital. When the issue was school management or mickey mouse, Town Meeting was perfunctory. However, as one member put it:

> "Even if an issue is mickey mouse, is it not the
> responsibility of an S.W.S. member to attend
> Town Meeting?"[33]

In this regard it is heartening that the community voted mandatory once weekly Town Meetings for 1977-78. This was a near unanimous vote of the sophomores and juniors, those who will be directly affected by the new policy. S.W.S. is, I believe, the first democratic school to do so by majority vote. Other such schools have not made mandatory attendance a matter of student choice or vote. My impression is that this decision reflected a more basic concern and commitment by the students and staff to build S.W.S. as a community, rather than to drift, or to end with a whimper.

In summary, at the end of Year 2, S.W.S. was well launched toward self-government. Most of the ingredients for that to happen were in place. Research was under way to document the effects of all of this on the students' moral and ego development. But the community and/or the consultants, for different reasons, may conclude that self-government isn't enough. Whether S.W.S. will, can, or should, opt for Dewey's much more profound conception of a democratic school then becomes a moot issue.

Assuming, for purposes of discussion, that S.W.S. chose to be a more democratic school what, in practical terms, might that mean? Again, recognizing that the answers would have to come, cooperatively, from discussion and decision by the community let me hazard some suggestions. A first need would be to identify and develop *more shared purposes*. These could be programs and activities (retreats, parties, athletics, drama, enrichment courses, community action, etc.) that cut across existing cliques and involve students in contacts with members they don't know. I think it would be useful for the community to debate and clarify what presently attracts kids to S.W.S., what the school stands for, in what

Ralph L. Mosher

ways it is an "alternative" and, most important, *how its programs and common purposes can be strengthened.* In this connection, I think the community should give serious consideration to *opening up S.W.S. to other groups of students* (e.g., to actively recruit more boys, blacks, and working class kids) so as to introduce more diversity and energy into the school.

Concurrently, I think that an effort to *expand S.W.S. as a caring community* - as a group that really cares about its members - would have positive effects. Retreats and the proposed advisory groups offering peer counseling, personal and academic support might be practical ways to accomplish this. The goal would be to make certain that being a member of S.W.S. means that one is treated as an individual - is truly known, cared about and supported by the faculty and many other students. To care deeply about other people (and to be cared for by them) is not only a developmental need for adolescents. It is a deep, persisting human and social need that is worth learning well.

Related to this is something the staff already does well, i.e., they individualize their relationships, teaching and counseling of the students. Students in S.W.S. are known and cared about personally and academically by the staff; their personal and scholastic development are monitored closely. The enrichment curriculum offers students the opportunity to pursue many special academic, artistic and other interests for credit. How much the enrichment curriculum depends on student initiative, or how much it is used by the staff and school as a planful way to individualize learning is less clear. Nonetheless, important elements - a scale of operation, teachers who know and care about students as individuals, and a flexible curriculum structure - are in place to permit genuine individualization of student learning and development, which is at the core of Dewey's conception of the democratic school.

Finally, it also seems critical, as the community had decided, *to keep self-governance going* and to expand the Town Meeting's focus to the major task of community building.

Part III, STAGE 5:
EVEN IF YOU CAN GET THERE, ISN'T ENOUGH

This section will summarize, *in general,* what we have learned from a modest effort during the two years, 1975-77, about developing self-governance in *one* alternative school. *First the good news*:

1) *These high school students can learn to govern themselves.* They can establish their own Robert's rules of order, make reasoned arguments and proposals, deliberate and legislate school policy on a variety of complex sensitive issues ranging from student evaluation (i.e., grading), moral development research at S.W.S., the appointment of new staff members and a school coordinator, the voting of mandatory Town Meetings (i.e., student governance of the school), etc. Nor do they finesse or avoid difficult issues (although dealing with what they see as arbitrary school authority exercised against them is easier than applying sanctions to irresponsibility by their own members). After two years of observing their weekly Town Meetings, it would be hard for me to say they govern themselves any less responsibly or democratically than do teachers, school committees, town meetings or university faculties I have known. That may sound cynical, or like damning with faint praise. It is not intended to be so at all. These students practice self-government with more good humor, forgiveness of their own frailties (as one student, rather generously, said to me: "I'm only 15, you're 45.") and light-heartedness than their elders. That may have something to do with the fact that I observe little covetousness or abuse of authority on their part. Self-government, it must be noted, is not a compelling interest to the majority of these alternative school students; its effects on their development (see point 3 below) are therefore restricted. I will turn shortly to an explanation of this as an artifact of their stage of development. The fact that many students are de-

faulted or indifferent citizens makes them no different, of course, than their parents. Hutchins has said precisely this - the average American is *not* a citizen. And, as noted, S.W.S. has voted mandatory participation in Town Meeting, in self-government of the school, for all its members in 1977-78. But the disinterest of many students, over the first two years, in school democracy defined as self-government must be acknowledged and faced.

2) I think it is valid to say that those *students who partici-pate in school democracy learn important parliamentary skills* - chairing meetings, speaking to the point, taking other students' views into account, etc. - which should generalize to their later lives. In fact, we don't know whether this happens. One can hope that an appetite for democratic decision making, and an attitude and understanding of its importance still persist. I strongly believe, however, a citizen-education case can be made that these students are learning, in Dewey's terms, to understand about self-government "the things that are done, that need to be done, and how to do them." And I think most objective observers would corroborate not only that the students become skillful parliamentarians but the practical utility of such training for American citizens.

3) Further, there is preliminary evidence that children and adolescents who participate in democratic (i.e., self-governing) classrooms or alternative schools show significant *gains in* their *measured moral reasoning.*[34] Such gains approach a half-stage increase in moral reasoning, roughly double the amount of gain achieved in most moral education courses within the existing curriculum. Much more comprehensive data to be collected longitudinally over the next two years on students at the School-Within-A-School, the Cluster School in Cambridge and the Civic Education units in Pittsburgh will clarify these highly preliminary, but promising, data as to the effects of a more democratic or just environment on moral and ego development. And

the data will be available for very different groups of adolescents. An extension of development and research in Brookline into the effects of democratic classrooms on younger children similarly will help to clarify Rundle's pioneering study with fifth-grade students. In addition, there is clinical evidence from the Cluster School that the incidence of stealing within the school has decreased very significantly - to the point where the students no longer steal from one another, nor in the larger school. This very tangible change in their moral behavior has not generalized to the "street," however. The issue of whether changes in students' moral reasoning has consequences for their behavior (in school and out of it) is obviously of great theoretical and practical importance. Barrett states the issue well - and the distance still to go - relative to the School-Within-A-School.

> "From my observations of Town Meeting, I do believe those students who participate are benefiting from the discussions and will, in fact, progress in moral stage development . . . However, what distresses me is that in their social interactions, I'm not at all sure there is carry over with regard to justice and fairness. There is a clique problem, a problem of exclusivity. I have not observed a great amount of cohesion, sensitivity, support and warmth exhibited in student relationships."[35]

Now (Second) to the Paradoxes

First, I believe that we need to avoid certain *definitional mistakes* in our research on school democracy:

a) For example, it would be easy to equate school democracy with studies of the effects on students of participating in the *governance* of alternative schools or classrooms. That may be as much or more than it is realistic, in the near term, to accomplish in most school democracy projects. But all of us need to do our homework on John Dewey. If our understanding of the truly democratic school is that it is a community providing the governance, social and educative conditions supportive of the *full* development of every student, then we will need to conceptualize and create such schools. Self-government will be but one aspect of such a school. . . .

b) And so will moral development. I believe it would be a mistake to reduce school democracy to a means (albeit a sophisticated one) to stimulate the moral development of students. God knows moral reasoning and behavior are critically missing in our present education of children and adolescents, but morality is not, repeat not, all there is to being human. Our "best" education has promoted idolatry of intellect;[36] idolatry of character or an obsession with justice, "a creeping moral developmentalism," would be similarly myopic. What we have to hold is a conception of a psychology and an education for whole and full human development.

c) I think there is a danger that we may focus too exclusively on efforts to democratize the school and pay insufficient attention to opportunities for learning about (and promoting) democracy in other institutions in the community. While I accept the dictum of "Physician - heal thyself" (i.e., educators should democratize schools first) Newmann's argument for education in democracy[37] and social action in the community is incontrovertible, as is Stanley's[38] pioneering study of educating families to be democratic.

Second, I believe there are real constraints which operate on democracy in school:

a) Students will understand and be democratic in qualitatively different ways depending on their stage of development. If stage theories have any validity at all, it follows that these points of view (whether moral or personal) significantly affect one's understanding of self-government, democracy, school rules, student rights and obligations, community, justice, etc. Further, any comprehensive understanding of Stage 5 would be one to three stages beyond most high school students, who tend to be a mix between Stage 2 and Stage 3 in Kohlberg's typology. Scharf[39] has illustrated the point in regard to students' different understanding of school rules and why they are essential. Interestingly, his illustration of Stage 4 reasoning ("rare in the schools we have observed") was drawn from an S.W.S. sophomore very active in the governance of the school: "In here it's important to enforce the rules so that everyone sees that they are respected. It's important to get everyone to come to Town Meeting so that the rules are seen as having real power. If people don't come they won't mean anything and it's better not to have them." This illustration underscores several points. Approximately 1/4 to 1/3 of the students at S.W.S. have given continuous leadership/commitment to school governance and the standing committees. They may be the students best able to understand and to state arguments about the complex moral and policy issues in governing the school and to see the importance of majority will as well as to tolerate the "mickey mouse" of management. Another 1/4 to 1/3 of the students were reasonably dutiful citizens (attended Town Meeting with some regularity, spoke infrequently). Nearly half the students, as noted, were marginal or non-participators. The relationship between participation in school governance and the student's stage of development is obviously a real issue in the vitality - general applicability - of such projects (as well as an empirical question on which we are now gathering data). And even when participation is mandatory, as it now is, we would expect the student's stage to de-limit his/her ability both to understand democracy and to be democratic.

Ralph L. Mosher

b) What we have said about the students applies as well to teachers. Most teachers are assumed to be at the conventional level of moral reasoning (Stages 3 and 4). Let us assume that they are a stage higher than high school students. This means that some of their thinking will incorporate Stage 5 and the need for majority will, consent freely given by all members of a community to the policies that will govern their institutional life together, etc. Certainly, we can expect many teachers to be genuinely attracted to the rhetoric of democracy. But a significant core of their thinking will have to do with authority, rule maintenance, discipline, the order of the school classroom (even if the issue becomes jealousness in defense of a new order, or disagreements as to who possesses the true gospel of the just community). The concept of a school where teachers know and care about one another, where the emphasis is on the quality of their relationships, may also figure prominently in the thinking of many teachers and counselors (for them, community is more important than democracy or justice). I do not disagree with this conception of community. I simply suggest its immanence, predictability (and appropriateness) because of the stage of the teachers in interaction with the students' thinking. Finally, those teachers whose thinking reflects the radical educators' passionate desire to liberate mankind from culture with its patterns and authority - who celebrate the individual and his/her freedom from the school - from any community obligations - "the free schoolers" - will be ambivalent about the obligations a democratic school will require of students for the common good.

What this says is that not all - perhaps not even a majority - of teachers will be comfortable with school democracy - or will have very different conception of it. All of the projects to date have encounted this issue:

"Two of the teachers had marked trouble dealing
with a more democratic classroom than they were
accustomed to. Hence, they vacillated between
permitting too much freedom and reverting to
directive teaching and strict, teacher-enforced
discipline. Both of these teachers had decided
by the end of the first semester that they did
not wish to return to the project next year."[40]

This observation underscores the essential nature of
teacher selection and education for projects in school
democracy.

c) As an extension of points a and b, it seems probable to
me that groups of students and teachers will create
*qualitatively different democratic schools or just com-
munities* depending on the predominant stage of moral
and ego development. Some of the possible differences
have already been alluded to. For example, I would expect a predominantly Stage 3 school to be much pre-
occupied with the students' social relationships with
some, but by no means all, peers and with the teachers.
Having and being with close friends; knowing teachers
intimately - "a more personal education" would be important reasons for belonging. I would expect such
students to be little troubled by school rules and teacher
authority which are seen as well-intentioned and personalized. One would work very hard, academically or
otherwise, to please and to be liked by such teachers
who know and care about him/her. Such a group might
be more likely to respond to an effort to create a caring
community - i.e., to expand the friendship group - to
add to the number of kids and faculty - "who know and
care about me" than to build a legislative, rule-main-
taining, self-governing community. The other side of
this could be that the school would be divided into
cliques, perhaps allied with particular teachers, to some
degree exclusive of one another and certainly so of out-

Ralph L. Mosher

siders. Self and peer group (one's sorority) would take precedence over the community as a whole; indeed, as noted, would be one's community. Further, a student's popularity or her attitude, rather than the rightness of her arguments or the objective "wrongness" of her school behavior could become critical in the community's decision-making, etc. Students would be loath to discipline friends or to bind them to broader community obligations, because one's social perspective and bond really only extend to one's immanent social group.

By contrast, students predominantly at Stage 4 understand that policy and rules are necessary for the school to exist as a community, that they protect the student's rights and freedoms as well as impartiality in discipline, that they have moral force and should be obeyed even if one's friends, teachers or parents will never know. There is a recognition that if the school, through Town Meeting, makes policy it has to be respected: "It's important to get everyone to come to Town Meeting so that the rules are seen as having real power." Otherwise, both the rules and the process of making them are subverted. Thus, the deliberation and deciding of school policy and rules is a serious business, even when its content is "mickey mouse." It is a critical process in identifying and legislating the common interests that bind the community. There is a realization that it is better for people to be authorities over themselves than to leave it to teachers (even trustworthy ones), and an intuitive sense that being in authority (for example, as Chairperson of Town Meeting, or as a member of a standing committee) can be rewarding. The obverse side of this may be an excess of debate, of speechmaking, of procedural rules or of legislation. This kind of procedural orgy can bore or frustrate many students or faculty.

(Peters argued in 1973 that the repetitiveness, tediousness and inefficiency of such exercises in self-government are an inevitable and worthwhile price to pay, because of the overall contribution being made to the students' education for democracy.)[41]

Regardless of the accuracy of these brief sketches of the ideological and practical differences in school democracy associated with predominant stage (and of which only two have been described), the point, hopefully, is clear. Both ways of understanding and practicing democracy/ community are likely to exist in experimental democratic high schools and classrooms; their relationship will be dialectical and will lead to development. For the educator the answer is "yes" to both. Each ideology is an authentic expression of a complex idea - in interaction and common cause they move a school one step further toward democracy.

d) The fact that schools are not now democratically organized or governed is a major and clear impediment to our efforts. Scharf states this problem well:

> "The increase in 'comprehensive' schools over the past thirty years implies a size and organization which makes meaningful democracy improbable. Schools of 2,000 or more are simply too large to have effective student participation. The division of the academic day by periods and subjects prohibits the development of a sense of community likely to make democracy plausible or desirable. Similarly, the hierarchial model of management found in comprehensive schools makes student participation likely to appear as a threat to the principal's political control of the school."[42]

This essay, already over-long, is not an anthology of all the constraints that operate on school democracy. But I have no doubt that the way in which, and the inertia with which public schools are presently managed, by professional "administrators" who set budgets, appoint

Ralph L. Mosher

and reward faculty, establish school regulations, administer discipline, adjudicate student rights, etc. is *the* major and formidable obstacle to all that this essay presages. (This happens, incidentally, under the muddy influence of systems development models copied from I.B.M. or the Harvard Business School). My sense, perhaps unfair, is that the rhetoric of school administration is Stage 4, with the actual management of schools being more characteristic of Stages 3, 2 and 1 in Kohlberg's typology.[43] To identify a problem is always easier than to create its solution, but to recognize it is a crucial first step. And it has consistently been my experience that there are many people in schools (including Headmasters, Assistant Superintendents, and Superintendents) who are just as professionally prescient as I and willing to try substantial, even systematic changes. That experience, after all, is part of my own democratic creed and commitment.

As a practical matter, we have miles to go before we sleep in understanding the complex consequences (and constraints) on school democracy experiments even at the present scale. Nor do we know how to vitalize representative school government, which is the predominant form of student government in the American high school. The question of the effective operational unit (the classroom, the alternative school, the "house," the student council) within the existing school in which to experiment with democracy is also moot.

My intuition is that the classroom is the most likely and practical place to promote democracy in the school. Why? Because it is of a size to permit individual participation and genuine common purposes, because it is the basic organizational unit of the school, and because much of what happens in classrooms goes on behind closed doors (i.e., is protected from management). Further, there is encouraging word as to what happens when elementary classrooms are democratic.[44] If we are not heard from for another two years, while others are espousing democracy as the new laetrile for schools, it will be, in part, because we are trying to learn more about both its promise and its problems in the classroom.

Epilogue:

Two points in conclusion. The first has to do with generating knowledge. I don't know whether the promise of school democracy (however defined) outweighs its problems. I do know that significant development in either individuals or institutions is not accomplished easily; and I know that we need much more educational research before the answers become clear. *I am unaware of any way to generate that knowledge except by more hard thinking and hard practice.* If such findings come first from unrealistically funded and supported experimental studies that may have to be so. Should cancer research stop because it is enormously costly and of uncertain outcome? The importance of research and development on democracy and its implications for education is incontrovertible. Our glass is sufficiently "half-full," in contrast to "half-empty," to warrant vigorous continuing study.

The last point is, for me, the most important of all. *A democratic education is one whose aim is the full development of every individual's potential.* Its psychology and its education must lead to whole people. It is unfortunate that that term has become cliched. Rationality, character, social contribution, the aesthetic, a sound body, emotion, work and soul are integral parts of human being and potential: the nine-fold helix that is everyone's birthright. For a variety of reasons - a sufficiency or insufficiency of psychological theory about one or another of these interrelated strands of development, a division of labor or the inability to keep a multi-variable model of human growth in mind - we may choose to practice a reductionism in either our psychological research or our educational development. But I can see no moral justification for limiting our conception of, or educational provision for, human potential. We need to persist in the effort to create the educational, social and governance conditions within and without our schools to support the full development of every person. Nor can we deny equal access to such an education, once it is practicable. *That* is the ultimate meaning of a democratic education.

REFERENCES and NOTES

1. Hutchins, Robert M., "The Unfinished Revolution. Is Democracy Possible?" *The Boston Globe*, (February 16, 1976).

2. Dewey, John. *Problems of Men*. (New York: Greenwood Press, 1968), p. 57.

3. Dewey, John. *Democracy and Education*. (New York: The Free Press, 1968), p. 99.

4. Newmann, Fred M. and Donald W. Oliver, "Education and Community," reprinted in David E. Purpel and Maurice Belanger, *Curriculum and the Cultural Revolution*. (Berkeley: McCutchan Publishing Corporation, 1972), p. 205.

5. Scharf, Peter, "School Democracy: Promise and Paradox." *Readings in Moral Education*. (Minneapolis: Winston Press, 1977).

6. Kateb, G., "Utopia and the Good Life." *Daedalus*, (Spring, 1965), p. 456.

7. Dewey, *op. cit.*, 1968, p. 69.

8. *Ibid.*, p. 61.

9. *Ibid.*, p. 50.

10. *Ibid.*, p. 52.

11. *Ibid.*, p. 48.

12. Gillespie, Judith A. and John J. Patrick. *Comparing Political Experiences*. (Washington: The American Political Science Association, 1974).

13. Dewey, *op. cit.*, pp. 62-63.

14. *Ibid.*, p. 59.

15. *Ibid.*, p. 14.

16. Dewey, John. *Reconstruction in Philosophy*. (New York: The American Library, 1950), p. 147.

17. Dewey, *Problems of Men*, pp. 63-64.

18. Lipset, Seymour Martin and William Schneider, "America's Schizophrenia on Achieving Equality." *Los Angeles Times,* (July 31, 1977).

19. Dewey, *op. cit.*, p. 66.

20. *Ibid.*, p. 113.

21. Locke, John. *Two Treatises of Government.* (New York: Hafner Publishing Company, 1956).

22. Ryan, Diane, "A Good Marriage." *At School in Brookline.* (Brookline,published by the School Committee, Summer, 1976). In a related way, S.W.S. is the first on-going school with a considerable, if unwritten history - in contrast to cluster schools or civic education classes created *de novo* - to adopt a democratic ideology in *mid stream.* The extent to which this new graft may take - especially as it grows counter to the school's roots in unbridled individualism - is informative.

23. DiStefano, Ann. Unpublished memorandum. (Brookline, School-Within-A-School, Parents Night, 1976).

24. *Ibid.*

25. Mosher, Ralph L., "A Three Year Democratic School Intervention Project." (Unpublished proposal to the Danforth Foundation, Boston University, 1976).

26. *Ibid.*, p. 4.

27. Wasserman, Elsa. *The Development of an Alternative High School Based on Kohlberg's Just Community Approach to Education.* (unpublished doctoral dissertation, Boston University, 1977).
Rundle, Louise. *Moral Development in the Fifth Grade Classroom.* (Unpublished doctoral dissertation, Boston University, 1977).

28. Kohlberg, L. and R. Mosher, "Brookline-Cambridge Moral Education Project: A Report of the Second Year, 1975-76." (Report to the Danforth Foundation, St. Louis, 1976).

29. Robert, Henry M. *Robert's Rules of Order.* (New York: Pyramid Books, 1973).

30. Fenton, Edwin, "The Pittsburgh Area Civic Education Project: A Report to the Danforth Foundation for the 1976-77 Fiscal Year." (Pittsburgh: Carnegie-Mellon University, 1977), p. 4.

31. Barrett, Diane, "The Just Community School Intervention Program, The School-Within-A-School, Brookline High School." (Unpublished paper, Boston University, 1977).

32. *Ibid.*

33. Finegold, Jordan, "Town Meeting: Is It Necessary?" *S.W.S. Newsletter*, (Brookline, Vol. 3,2, 1977).

34. Wasserman and Rundle, *ops. cit.*

35. Barrett, *op. cit.*

36. McGeorge Bundy, the former Dean of Harvard College, writing in *Daedalus*, said: "I will assert that we were right on one absolutely vital point, we know what education was for, learning. The university is for learning - not for politics, not for growing up, not even for virtue."

37. Newmann, Fred M. *Education for Citizen Action: Challenge for Secondary Schools.* (Berkeley: McCutchan Publishing Corporation, 1972).

38. Stanley, Sheila. *A Curriculum to Affect the Moral Atmosphere of the Family and the Moral Development of Adolescents.* (Unpublished doctoral dissertation, Boston University, 1975).

39. Scharf, *op. cit.*

40. Fenton, *op. cit.,* p. 3.

41. Peters, Richard S. *Authority, Responsibility and Education.* (London: George Allen and Unwin, Ltd., 1973).

42. Scharf, *op. cit.*, p. 11.

43. For example, a handbook on Student Rights distributed by the California State Board of Education identifies Student Rights in the areas of corporal punishment, classroom prayer, sex discrimination and search and seizure of student property. Significantly, however, the Handbook tells students they "must pursue the required course of study and submit to the authority of the teacher of the school."

44. See Rundle, *op. cit.*, Stuhr's article in the issue and Thomas Lickona, "Creating the Just Community with Children," *Theory Into Practice*, Volume XVI, 2, April, 1977.

APPENDIX

Table I, Change Data Across One Year for Ten Students in the School Within a School in Brookline, Massachusetts: 1977-1978.

Student Grade-Level:	Year in School Within a School:	1977 Data ---		1978 Data ---		Changes (1977-1978)	
		Stage Score:	MMS:	Stage Score:	MMS:	Stage Score:	MMS:
10th	1st (new)	3(2)	280	3(4)	325	+ 1/2	+ 45
10th	1st	3	300	3(4)	345	+ 1/3	+ 45
11th	1st	3	300	4(3)	367	+ 2/3	+ 67
11th	2nd	3(2)	262	3(4)	336	+ 1/2	+ 74
11th	1st (new)	4(3)	379	3(4)	333	- 1/3	- 46
11th	2nd	4(3)	350	4(3)	369	000	+ 19
11th	1st	3	300	4(3)	371	+ 2/3	+ 71
11th	2nd	3	300	3(4)	320	+ 1/3	+ 20
11th	1st (new)	3(4)	328	4	383	+ 1/2	+ 55
11th	2nd	4	413	4	381	000	- 32
COLUMN MEANS:			321		353	+ 1/3 Stage	+ 32 MMS

- -

WHERE: Stage Score = Measure of Moral Development (Kohlberg)

MMS = Moral Maturity Score (Kohlberg)

- -

Table I is based on preliminary data supplied by Ralph L. Mosher; April, 1978.

- -

Ralph L. Mosher

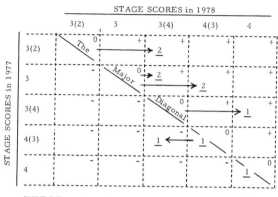

STAGE SCORES in 1978

WHERE:

Underlined numbers represent frequencies.

0 represents no change in Stage Score.

+ represents an increase in Stage Score.

- represents a decrease in Stage Score.

Figure 1, Change in Stage Scores for Ten Students in the School Within a School in Brookline, Massachusetts: Preliminary Results Across the Calendar Year 1977-1978.

NOTE: 1. All seven (7) students that began in 1977 with a predominance of Stage 3 moral reasoning (i. e., Stages 3(2), 3, and 3(4)) moved toward Stage 4 moral reasoning. Each of these students gained between 1/3 to 2/3 of a Stage in their moral reasoning.

2. The three (3) students that began in 1977 with a predominance of Stage 4 moral reasoning (i. e., Stages 4(3) and 4) did not show any positive change across a year's time. This result suggests that Stage 4 moral reasoning may be a ceiling for the development of moral reasoning in the Brookline School Within a School.

Figure 1 is based on preliminary data supplied by Ralph L. Mosher; April, 1978.

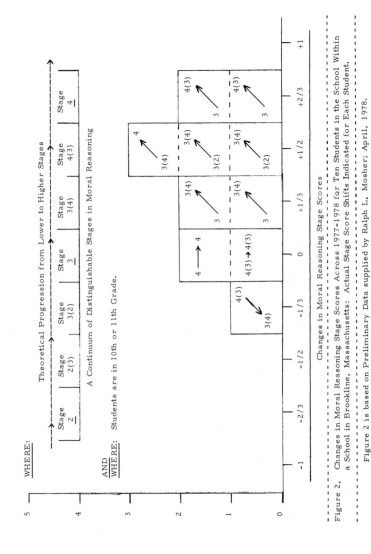

Figure 2, Changes in Moral Reasoning Stage Scores Across 1977–1978 for Ten Students in the School Within a School in Brookline, Massachusetts: Actual Stage Score Shifts Indicated for Each Student.

Figure 2 is based on Preliminary Data supplied by Ralph L. Mosher; April, 1978.

Ralph L. Mosher

Psychological and Moral Development for Teachers: Can You Teach Old Dogs?

Sharon N. Oja
Norman A. Sprinthall

INTRODUCTION

As Sprinthall and Mosher noted in their article, programs for educational reform and "new education" have typically focused on either the pupil or new curriculum materials. Teachers, the third part of the educational triangle, have usually been viewed in static terms. Educators often speak of pupil growth and development, or of stimulating classroom materials. Yet, when it comes to teachers, there is either an attempt to make the curriculum teacher-proof, like learning to paint by the numbers, or to provide teachers with brief low-level skill training and hope for the best. Neither effort has been successful. The great national teacher-proof curriculum projects of the 60's have all faded almost totally into the obscurity of school file rooms and desk drawers, quietly gathering dust. The efforts of a brief skills-only education for in-service teachers have been episodic and equally ineffective. The results of a massive national review of in-service teacher education by Joyce, Howey and Yarger provide a discouraging and depressing account of failure.[1] The study included interview data from more than 1000 school personnel, community, congressional and state department members. Also some 2000 volumes, 600 journal articles, and major position papers were reviewed. These multiple sources of information all tend to refer to in-service teacher education with negative connotations. There are over-all feelings of skepticism, discontent, and dissatisfaction resulting in the description of the in-service teacher education effort as "weak," "impoverished," and as a "relative failure." [2]

These reactions parallel the general flavor of earlier reviews of education such as those by Getzels and Jackson,[3] Cyphert and Spaights,[4] and Biddle and Ellena.[5] This, in spite of careful documentation which indicates that there are massive numbers of personnel involved in the effort of in-service education (e.g., some one-quarter of a million, at the last count). To praphrase Winston Churchill: It can be said of teacher education that never have so many worked so hard to produce so little.

THEORY FOR TEACHER EDUCATION

In our view, a major source of difficulty in this area has been the lack of coherent theory and practice for teacher education. We know that one cannot really teacher-proof materials, nor can brief skills-only training produce lasting change. On the latter point, there is ample research evidence that learning a few discrete skills, such as microteaching and/or microcounseling does not transfer to the classroom. The surface skills wash out and the teacher quickly resumes practice as usual.[6]

The lack of theory, as Shutes points out, is a prime consideration in this dismal picture.[7] Teacher education, he suggests, is guided at best by fragmented, capricious bits of folk-wisdom, unevaluated and non-cumulative experience. The result then is not surprising: Practice without theory growing first in one direction, then another, wandering aimlessly between the trivial and the cosmic, and not knowing the difference. Slogans and statements *ex cathedra* such as "Competency-Based Teacher Education" are simply current examples of a long history of atheoretical eclecticism in teacher education.

The current study is an attempt to reverse the trend and to establish a research base including a coherent theory, and

118   Oja and Sprinthall

systematic practice; obviously a tall order. Yet, we have discerned in the past decade a small but increasing base or beachhead for such work.

STRANDS AND CONTRIBUTIONS FOR DEVELOPMENTAL TEACHER EDUCATION

Extrapolating from our work with children and teenagers, we confronted the question: Can the framework also hold for adults? Developmental theory posits such concepts as growth through stages, qualitative change, an invariant and hierarchical sequence. What would happen if we applied these to adults? Could we conceptualize teacher growth as a dependent variable? As with children and teenagers, could we attempt to create a developmental learning environment designed to stimulate personal/professional growth or (more formally) cognitive structural change on the part of the teacher?

Cognitive development (including the ego, the conceptual, and the moral domains) is based on the presupposition that how complexly persons *think and feel* is governed by their stage of development. In its barest form then, what such a framework posits for teacher education is simply that if we wish teachers to perform more adequately, programs are needed to stimulate teachers' development to yet higher, more complex stages.

The seminal research of O. J. Harvey, Schroeder and David Hunt[8] has recently provided a key empirical and theoretical bridge connecting developmental concepts to classroom teaching. They were able to document through natural setting research that teachers who were classified at more advanced developmental stages were more effective as classroom teachers. Given the long, dreary and inconsequential research history in teacher effectiveness, this work was a clear breakthrough. Stated simply, teachers at higher stages of development functioned in the classroom at a more complex level (e.g., they were more adaptive in teaching style, flexible and tolerant). Also, such teachers were more responsive to individual differences and, most importantly, employed a variety of teaching models (e.g., lectures, small discussions, role-plays, indirect teaching strategies) and were more empathic; that is, such teachers could accurately "read" and respond to the emotions of their pupils. From a theoretical perspective this is reasonable, since at higher stages humans are capable of multiple perspective-taking. Their perceptual field is broad or (in Witkin's term) such teachers are field independent versus field dependent.[9] In sum, such teachers provide an abundant learning environment for their pupils.

While Harvey, Hunt and others have demonstrated the crucial relationships between developmental stage and teacher performance, they have not taken the next step. Can we build educational programs which will stimulate the teacher's level of development? At present, research can identify both pre-service and in-service teachers who are at various developmental levels. However, there have been no attempts to explore whether or not it is possible to change and improve the developmental stages of teachers. In one sense, this is a curious omission, since there is such an overwhelming body of research documenting both the modest psychological/ego/moral developmental level of adults in general (including teachers) and the ineffective level of instruction in most of the classrooms of this country. Studies as far back as 1912 and as recent as 1975 indicate that, in most classrooms, teachers do 80% of the talking and use only one mode of instruction.[10] Thus, the need for change is obvious and, with the basic work of O. J. Harvey, David Hunt and others at hand, the needed theoretical framework is available.

One final theoretical point. A colleague of Hunt's, Edward Sullivan, was the first to extend the theoretical framework into broader areas.[11] Hunt, of course, was mostly concerned about stages of conceptual development, how a person thinks about educational issues, learning, knowledge, etc. Sullivan was able to demonstrate that this was one domain of developmental stage theory and that conceptual stages were related to ego stage (Loevinger) and moral-ethical stage (Kohlberg). This broadened the developmental perspective. The framework became more inclusive and comprehensive representing a variety of developmental domains: the personal, the ethical and the conceptual (and with Selman's most recent work we can add, the interpersonal). Sullivan, then, provided a most important expansion of theory by pushing it to the broader Deweyian notion of a whole person processing experience through a variety of overlapping developmental domains.

THE STUDY

As a result we decided to create an educational program for teachers, employing a developmental education format (the so-called balanced-curriculum, role-taking, disequilibrating). Also, we focused on developmental stage change of teachers as our dependent variable as measured by three different yet overlapping instruments - - the Hunt Conceptual Level Test, the Rest DIT of Moral Development, and the Loevinger Test of Ego Development.

Participants for this study were in-service elementary and secondary school teachers and other student support personnel (counselors, social workers) who were enrolled in summer school classes in the College of Education at the University of Minnesota. The experimental subjects participated in a special Developmental Education workshop offered for regular graduate credits. The control subjects were enrolled in various other education courses. The instructional staff consisted of six doctoral students and two faculty members in the Developmental Education Program.

Standardized measures of the independent variable, personal psychological development in the stages of ego, moral and conceptual growth, were administered to both experimental and comparison groups on a pretest-posttest basis. Professional/skill acquisition was measured for only the experimental group by a facilitative counseling measure similar to Gazda and Carkhuff and the Flanders indirect teaching analysis system.[12] The communication skill measure was administered at the beginning of the summer workshop in June, at the end of the summer workshop in July, and at the end of the fall practicum in December. Audio tapes of classroom teaching in May, before the summer workshop, and in December, during the fall practicum, formed the measure of indirect teaching for one sub-group of experimental teachers.

CURRICULUM OBJECTIVES

General objectives of the curriculum for the adult teachers included (1) the development of more complex, differentiated, and integrated understanding of self and others, (2) increased cognitive complexity, (3) development toward principled morality, and (4) increase in knowledge of educational psychology and increased skills in communication. The program used three instructional settings: large group didactic learning, small group laboratory learning, and fall quarter practicum application. The curriculum existed in three phases:

Phase I - Building supportive interpersonal relationships within the small groups to facilitate developmental growth.

Phase II - Learning the skills of facilitative teaching, indirect teaching, and individualizing instruction in addition to the content of cognitive-developmental theory.

Phase III - Applying the skills and theory to the real classroom setting with significant on-going supervision.

The workshop in the summer concentrated on Phases I and II of the curriculum while Phase III, the ongoing supervision of the practicum, occurred during the fall quarter of the year as teachers returned to their classrooms to try out mini-units based on their newly acquired skills and theory.

The summer workshop ran from 8:30 to 12:00, four days a week for five weeks. Each day was divided into a large group session, 8:30-10:00, and a small group session, 10:30-12:00. The large group dealt mainly in didactic learning (lectures and discussions) specifically relating principles and theories of human development (Elkind, Erikson, Loevinger, Hunt, Kohlberg, Piaget and Perry) and principles of behavioral contracting to adults' personal development, social roles, and educational practice in classrooms (including individualizing instruction and mainstreaming). Small group sessions each day focused on learning and practicing facilitative communication skills and group process skills, with particular emphasis on the personal/professional identity issues of adults. Additionally, the adult teachers focused on transferring the theory and skills to the classrooms through the planning of three required mini-units to be implemented in the fall practicum. These were aimed to encourage teachers to see the multiple perspectives in their roles (e.g., as indirect teacher, as group facilitator, as supportive supervisor and as counselor within the classroom), and to experience a variety of possibilities in relating to students as well as to other adults in the educational system. The four focus points of developmental approaches to learning existed within all three phases of the curriculum. They were (1) *seminar approach with practicum experience*—the "action plus reflection" framework; (2) *significant social role-taking*—the ability to take the perspective of others; (3) *on-going supervision;* and (4) *provision for support* during times of disequilibrium in new learning.

RESULTS

The study employed three empirical measures of developmental stage, the Loevinger, the Rest, and the Hunt. Since there are no single valid measures, an overlapping assessment was employed with the three tests serving as proximate measures. The results will be presented in the following order: Loevinger, Rest and Hunt. Each is viewed as an indicator of how each person processes or makes meaning from experience by developmental level. The Loevinger largely assesses how an individual thinks about or conceptualizes about self; the Rest assesses how a person processes social-justice questions; the Hunt assesses how a person conceptualizes issues of teaching and learning.

EGO DEVELOPMENT

Table I indicates the results of independent t-tests comparing the mean ego level score of the experimental to the comparison group on both pretest and posttests. No significant differences were found on the pretest scores between the two groups.

TABLE I,	LOEVINGER EGO DEVELOPMENT SCORES for Both a Pretest and a Posttest of Experimental vs. Control Groups.					
VARIABLE:	N grp:	SC-18 a Mean:	S. D.:	d. f.:	Value of t:	Probability:
Pretests --						
Experimental	30	6.867	0.681	53	n. s. b	
Comparison	25	6.720	0.678			
Posttests --						
Experimental	30	6.900	0.662	53	1.70	.01 p .05 c
Comparison	25	6.560	0.821			

WHERE:

a = Loevinger's SC-18 ego level scores have been transformed into a 1-10 interval value according to the following convention:

Ego level:	1	2	Δ	Δ3	3	3/4	4	4/5	5	6
Interval value:	1	2	3	4	5	6	7	8	9	10

b = Since the pretesting is designed to assess whether or not the two groups are derived from the same population, a two-tailed test of probability is appropriate, and was used.

c = Since the posttesting is designed to assess whether the Experimental group is higher in score than the Control (or Comparison) group and, so, involves testing a prediction of direction, a one-tailed test of probability is appropriate, and was used.

Posttest scores indicate that the Experimental Group Mean was significantly different from the Control. Since developmental theory predicts direction for change, a one-tailed test of significance was employed. The computed posttest t was 1.70 and with 53 NDF this was significant beyond the .05 level. Inspection of the mean scores in *Table I*, however, revealed that the source of significance was probably derived more from the decrease on posttest by the Control group than an increase by the Experimentals group. In fact, the decline in posttest scoring is apparently the general expectation when employing the Loevinger with adult populations.[13] Thus, the Control group regressed in scoring (as do most adults on a pre/post basis) while the Experimental group essentially remained stable. This cannot be taken, however, as a major indicator of developmental growth. At best, it can be considered a trend. On an overall basis, the Experimental group remained at Stage 5 on the Loevinger, a highly stable adult stage of development and similar to Kohlberg's Stage 4.

MORAL/ETHICAL DEVELOPMENT

The Defining Issues Test from Rest,[14] attempts to assess what people see as crucial moral issues in a situation by presenting subjects with a moral dilemma and a list of definitions of the major issues involved. In this study for each of three stories (dilemmas), subjects evaluated a set of twelve issues and were asked to rate how important each issue is in deciding what ought to be done, and to rank their choices of the four most important issues. Since each issue statement represents a moral judgment stage, a subject's choices of the most important issues over a number of moral dilemmas are taken as a measure of his/her grasp of different stages of moral reasoning. The P (Principled Thinking) score is the sum of the subject's Stage 5A, 5B, and 6 usage scores in Kohlbergian terms.

Table II indicates that there was no significant difference between the two groups on the DIT pretest. Both groups can be considered as being drawn from the same population of adult teachers. The table also indicates that the two groups were statistically significantly different on posttest scores (18.3 versus 14.9), a difference favoring the experimentals.

TABLE II,   REST "PRINCIPLED MORAL THOUGHT" SCORES (Percent & Raw) from the Defining Issues Test for Both a Pretest & a Posttest of Experimental vs. Control Groups.[a]

VARIABLE:	N grp	DIT-3 Means -- Raw:[b]	Percent:[b]	S.D.:	d.f.:	Value of t:	Prob.:
Pretests --							
Experimental	27	16.33	56.3%	4.56			
					46	1.81	n.s.[c]
Comparison	21	13.43	46.3%	6.59			
Posttests --							
Experimental	27	18.296	63.1%	0.959			
					46	2.06	0.02[d]
Comparison	21	14.952	51.5%	1.372			

WHERE:

[a] = In this study a three-story/dilemma form of Rest's DIT was used.

[b] = In order to transfer from a raw score to a percent score, simply divide the raw score by the constant 29.

[c] = Since the pretesting is designed to assess whether or not the two groups are derived from the same population, a two-tailed test of probability is appropriate, and was used.

[d] = Since the posttesting is designed to assess whether the Experimental group is higher in score than the Control (or Comparison) group and, so, involves testing a prediction of direction, a one-tailed test of probability is appropriate, and was used.

The results indicate that experimental teachers (N = 27) gained significantly pre to post in their use of principled moral thinking. The experimental teachers increased their average score on the DIT-3 test from 56.3% to 63.1%, which represents a percentage increase significant at P = .018 (two-tailed test). This compares favorably with Bernier's results with in-service teachers (N = 16) which showed an increase from 56.8% to 65.8% (p < .01, two-tailed).[15]

The comparison subjects (N = 21) showed no significant shift on the DIT-3 in this study.

CONCEPTUAL DEVELOPMENT

Conceptual Level (CL) is a measure of cognitive complexity as well as learning style according to Hunt.[16] Scores range from 0 to 3 and a higher score indicates more complexity in processing information, greater interpersonal maturity, and a learning style requiring less structure. The test is a six item paragraph completion test, similar in format to the Loevinger.

The results are presented in *Table III* and indicate that the Experimental and Comparison groups were not significantly different in mean pretest scores. Comparison on the posttest, however, revealed a statistically significant difference (p = .013), indicating the posttest experimental mean CL score was significantly higher than that of the Comparison group.

TABLE III, HUNT CONCEPTUAL LEVEL TEST SCORES (Raw Score Means) for Both a Prestest and a Posttest of an Experimental Group vs. a Control Group: Data from Administrations of Hunt's Paragraph Completion Test of Conceptual Level.

VARIABLE:	N grp	MEANS:[a]	S. D.:	d. f.:	Value of t:	Prob.:
Pretests --						
Experimental	31	1.855	0.290	52	---	n. s.[b]
Comparison	23	1.696	0.372			
Posttests --						
Experimental	31	2.010	0.375	52	2.29	0.013[c]
Comparison	23	1.787	0.322			

WHERE:

[a] = Hunt's Paragraph Completion Test of Conceptual Level generates scores that can range from 0 to 3. Scores of 1, 2 or 3 on this test may be interpreted as indicating the following conceptual levels:

Score of 1 = Categorical judgments, stereotyped thought. Other directed; accepts single rules.

Score of 2 = Self delineation, awareness of alternatives, & awareness of emotions.

Score of 3 = Abstract internal principles, awareness of multiple viewpoints.

[b] = Since the pretesting is designed to assess whether or not the two groups are derived from the same population, a two-tailed test of probability is appropriate, and was used.

[c] = Since the posttesting is designed to assess whether the Experimental group is higher in score than the Control (or Comparison) group and, so, involves testing a prediction of direction, a one-tailed test of probability is appropriate, and was used.

The three empirical estimates of stage growth indicate that the workshop experience apparently stimulated some developmental change, yet the results were not completely consistent. On the estimates of ethical reasoning and conceptual thought, the workshop teachers achieved scores which were statistically different from their colleagues in regular summer school courses. On the other hand, in terms of their general stage of ego development, there was apparently no immediate shift. If the Loevinger is viewed as the most general measure of adult personality (which the theorist does in fact claim), then the workshop may not have been either long enough nor intense enough to engender a major stage shift from Stage 4 to 5. As Mosher's paper details, such a shift apparently requires a major change in the entire educational environment, including how the school as a system is organized.

The pattern of interaction between teacher and pupil, teacher and teacher, and teacher and administrator must shift to the level of general democratic principles or so-called "just communities." The fact that our workshop did not go beyond the classroom as it currently exists may account for the lack of over-all change. Self-contained classrooms traditionally clustered may represent a ceiling (or lid) on the amount of developmental change that is possible. The upward shift in ethical and conceptual thinking would theoretically improve the learning atmospheres in somewhat conventional classrooms. Teachers, as well as participant observers, reported this to be the case. The workshop teachers tended to become less dictatorial and arbitrary, on one hand, and more indirect and empathic, on the other.

Table IV presents the results of the workshop teachers' ability to accurately identify and respond to human emotions over the period of the program. *Table V* reports the available data on one sub-group of workshop teachers who provided pre-posttest tapes of their actual classroom teaching. This indicates that they improved in their ability to employ the dimensions of indirect teaching, which Flanders' research has documented as a more effective mode than the traditional directive approach to teaching.[17] Thus, in *Table V*, the data indicate that the elementary teachers shifted from 59% direct instruction (or 41% indirect) to 43% direct (or 57% indirect). This is a significant shift. Extensive research by Flanders and his associates has shown that teachers talk about 60% of the time in classrooms, a finding incidentally that has remained almost constant since studies of the phenomena began in 1912, as we noted earlier.

TABLE IV, REFLECTION OF FEELING SCORES and CORRELATED T-TEST VALUES for Only the Experimental Group (N= 32).

VARIABLE:	N_{grp}:	MEANS:[a]	S. D. :	d. f. :	Value of t:	Prob. :
Administrations, Time of: Exp. Grp.[b]						
T_1 (first)	32	2.003	0.601	31	-7.66	.001[c]
T_2 (second)	32	2.691	0.482			
T_1 (first)	32	2.003	0.601	31	-5.75	.001[c]
T_3 (third)	32	2.594	0.629			
T_2 (second)	32	2.691	0.482	31	1.29	0.208
T_3 (third)	32	2.594	0.629			

WHERE:

[a] = The workshop teachers' ability to accurately identify and respond to human emotions (over the period of the program) were rated on a 1-5 scale, on which the scale-points meant the following --

Score of 1 = Total lack of awareness of emotions;
Score of 2 = Awareness, but slight distortion of feelings;
Score of 3 = Accurate identification & response to feelings;
Score of 4 = Goes beyond the stated content & feelings that are expressed (e. g. , Leads);
Score of 5 = Goes well beyond expressed feelings (e. g. , Suggests major new awareness to subject).

[b] = The "Times of Administration" for the instrument that generated the Reflection of Feeling scores are defined as follows --

T_1 (first) = Beginning of the Summer Workshop.
T_2 (second) = Conclusion of the Summer Workshop.
T_3 (third) = Conclusion of the follow-up Fall Practicum.

[c] = Since the correlated t-Test is for the same group, with only time of administration varied, and the intent is to assess whether or not change has taken place within the group on the measure used, a two-tailed test of probability is appropriate, and was used.

TABLE V, INDIRECT TEACHING LEVELS and CORRELATED T-TEST VALUES for a Sub-Sample of the Experimental Group Who Provided Pretest/Posttest Tapes of Their Classroom Teaching.

VARIABLE:	N grp.	MEANS:[a]	S.D.:	d.f.:	Value of t:	Prob.:[b]
Pretests --	10	0.412				
			0.195	09	-3.27	less than 0.01
Posttests --	10	0.573				

WHERE:

[a] = Reported Means are for the Indirect Ratio, which is calaculated from data using the Flanders categories. The Indirect Ratio is itself calculated by adding Flanders' categories 1 through 4 and, then, dividing that sum by the sum of the Flanders categories 1 through 7.

[b] = Since the correlated t-Test is for the same group (or, more precisely, the same sub-group of the total Experimental Group), with essentially time of teaching behavior varied, and the intent is to assess whether or not change across that time period on the measure used has taken place, a two-tailed test of probability is appropriate, and was used.

Other, more clinically oriented assessments of the program tended to confirm the empirical findings. The teachers rated the program highly in self-report questionnaires, with positive ratings between 5 and 6 on a 7-point scale. They also indicated in their weekly journals their growing confidence and success in implementing some of the new skills into their classroom. We had asked them to implement "mini-units" in peer counseling, cross-age teaching and individualizing instruction as a method to increase their repertoire of teaching skills. They were not always successful, but their discussion of both success and failure indicated a broader perception of their pupils and an increase in their own self-analytic skills.

IMPLICATIONS

As noted at the outset of this article, we have deliberately selected a most difficult and complex issue for a research investigation. Thus, it is not surprising that the first set of results are somewhat inconclusive. Our earlier studies with children and teenagers were similarly promising, yet, far from definitive. The present study has a number of obvious implications. Creating effective developmental experiences for adults is substantially more complex than for children and adolescents. In one sense, this is easy to understand. Adults tend to stabilize into consistent and somewhat impervious stages. Somewhat quaintly, William James referred to this as "old fogeyism;"[18] namely, the tendency for adults to avoid significant change, to process new experience in familiar terms, and to avoid significantly new perceptions. In the specific case of adults as teachers, we've already noted the remarkable consistency of teaching style, not only within, but across generations. A recent study of educational change by the Rand Corporation reviewed a decade of innovative programs. There was almost no transfer. As soon as the funds were withdrawn, business as usual returned. "It was a universal experience of these projects that, regardless of their degree of success, they were studiously ignored by their colleagues—(even if) the school may have been a virtual Walden III . . . ."[19]

However, we do not wish to plead that the problems are too great and, therefore, we should be excused from further effort. Instead, our view is that (in a major sense) we need to build new programs through a gradual process of action and reflection. This initial study does provide some foundation. Teachers can learn theory and skills which, at least, partially impact their stage of development. It may be that the next step is to work more comprehensively on applications to their own classrooms. Possibly, this could include the creation of more democratic classrooms (in the Dewey sense). It may be unrealistic to foresee entire school systems opting à la Mosher for "just high schools." Yet, individual teachers, class by class, may be able to restructure their own learning environments to promote and stimulate pupil growth.

At this point, we simply don't know either what is possible or what is requisite to provide interactive learning environments for both teachers and pupils. A developmental framework does indicate that such educational problems cannot be solved in isolation. Consecutiveness and interaction are required. Pupils teachers, and curriculum materials are equal participants in either educational growth or stalemate.

Our studies with children and teenagers indicate that growth can occur under conditions of significant experience and careful reflection. Gradually inducing *more* complex role-taking and *more* self reflection form the parameters of developmental education. The present study, while raising many unanswered questions, does support the possibility that what is true for pupil growth may be true for adults as well. In the long run, then, further study in this area may uncover and illuminate theory and practice for adult professional growth and development.

The concept of cognitive structural change, the process through which humans move from the less complex to the more complex in a variety of developmental domains, remains a compelling framework for our work. The classic dictum in education states, "As is the teacher so is the school." Perhaps in the future we can say, "As the teacher becomes, so the schools grow."

REFERENCES

1. Joyce, B., K. Howey and S.Yarger. *Issues to Face. Report One: In Service Teacher Education.* (Palo Alto, California: Education Research and Development Center, 1976.)

2. *Ibid.*

3. Getzels, J. and P. Jackson, "The Teachers Personality and Characteristics." In N. Gage (Ed.) *Handbook of Research on Teaching.* (Chicago: Rand McNally, 1964.)

4. Cyphert, F. and E. Spaights. *An Analysis and Projection of Research in Teacher Education.* (Columbus: Ohio State University Research Press, 1964.)

5. Biddle, B. and W. Ellena. *Contemporary Research on Teacher Effectiveness.* (New York: Holt, Rinehart and Winston, 1964.)

6. MacDonald, F. A., "A Behavior Modification View of Video Playback: Micro-teaching." Paper presented at AERA National Convention, New Orleans, March, 1973.

7. Schutes, R. E., "Needed: A Theory of Teacher Education." In *Texas Tech Journal of Education* (2, 1975), pp. 94-101.

8. Harvey, O. J., D. E. Hunt and H. M. Schroder. *Conceptual Systems and Personality Organization.* (New York: John Wiley and Sons, Inc., 1961.)

9. Witkin, H. A. *Personality through Perception.* (New York: Harper, 1953.)

10. See Chapters 2, 10 and 14 in R. C. Sprinthall and N. A. Sprinthall, *Educational Psychology: A Developmental Approach.* (Reading, Massachusetts: Addison-Wesley, 1977.)

11. See particularly E. V. Sullivan, et. al., "A Developmental Study of the Relationship Between Conceptual, Ego and Moral Development." In *Child Development* (41, 1970), pp. 399-411.

12. We created a system to assess so-called "accurate empathy" based on a synthesis of work by R. A. Carkhuff, *Human Resource Development* (New York: Holt, Rinehart and Winston, 1967), and G. Gazda, *Human Relations Development* (Boston: Allyn and Bacon, 1973), and the Flanders system — see N. A. Flanders, *Analyzing Teacher Behavior*, (Reading, Massachusetts: Addison-Wesley, 1970).

13, Loevinger, J. *Ego Development.* (San Francisco: Jossey-Bass, 1976.)

14. Rest, J. *The Defining Issues Test.* (Burton Hall, University of Minnesota, Minneapolis, Minnesota 55455, 1974.)

15. Bernier, J. *A Psychological Education Intervention for Teacher Development.* (Unpublished doctoral dissertation, University of Minnesota, 1976.)

16. Hunt, D. and E. Sullivan. *Between Psychology and Education.* (New York: Dryden Press, 1974.)

17. Flanders, *op. cit.*

18. James, William. *Talks with Teachers.* (New York: Norton, 1958.)

19. Mann, D., "The Politics of Training Teachers in Schools," in *The Teachers College Record* (77, 3, 1976), p. 337.

Values Education and American Schools: Worlds in Collision?

Paul J. Sullivan
Mary F. Dockstader

Schools are under more pressure today than at any other time in recent memory. The apparent decline in college board and other standardized test scores, the decreasing value of high school and college diplomas in obtaining jobs, the rising absentee rates, the increase of vandalism and violence in the schools, and a general sense that "something is wrong" with education are eroding public confidence in the schools. Television specials, national magazines and newspapers all describe the problems and inquire into their causes. The reasons, however, are complex and rooted as much in society as in the schools. But the school presents a convenient target.

This questioning attitude toward education has led citizens in many cities and towns to turn down school funding requests. Entire school systems have closed for days, weeks or months because of lack of money. The public no longer automatically provides money for education. The doubt and alienation felt by many people is expressed by this lack of support for the schools.

At the same time, there is a growing movement for "accountability" and "back to the basics" in education. Concepts like management by objectives (MBO) are borrowed from business and applied to education with slight adaptation. Many states have adopted statewide testing programs, mandated learner objectives and regulated schools more closely. This tendency has accelerated as states have increased their financial support of education. In the state of Washington, for example, the special levy election system of funding education is being replaced by state government funding as a result of a court order. But at the same time, the legislature is mandating that learner objectives be written and implemented in grades 1 - 12. This is coupled with an extensive statewide testing program.

A vocal minority that has gained substantial attention is the group that demands a return to the basics. They want the schools to focus almost exclusively on the "3 R's;" to provide more discipline, more drill, more recitation, more homework and more testing; to eliminate "frills," such as electives and the school's social services; and to ban innovations in curriculum. Facts, not concepts, must be taught. This listing is, of course, a composite of the demands put forward by various individuals supporting the back-to-basics movement.

One belief these individuals have in common is a feeling that, somehow, things were better at some indeterminant time in the past. But they do not address a number of fundamental issues. Where is "back"? What is "basic"? Especially, what is "basic" for the 1970's and the 1980's? What knowledge and skills are of the most worth? Careful consideration has not been given to these questions either by many of the back-to-basics critics of education or by their supporters. H. L. Mencken once said that there is always an easy answer to every problem: one that is neat, plausible and *wrong.* One must wonder if this is not another case of looking for such an easy answer to an uncommonly complex problem.

Within this larger framework of doubt about the schools is the question of their role in values or moral education. Public concern for this aspect of children's educational experience has grown in recent years. The Watergate scandal with its cast of intelligent, well-educated individuals who knew or cared little about personal and political ethics was one national crisis which aroused people's concern for values and moral decision-making. Large corporations have made illegal campaign contributions and bribed foreign governments to gain advantages over competitors. Congressmen have also been suspected of accepting bribes from Korean representatives.

These highly publicized national events occurred at the same time that medicine, science, politics and rapidly changing social conditions have been presenting us with new, perplexing moral questions which must be resolved. These questions range from the very personal to issues which could affect the survival of mankind. The *pace* of change and the sheer *volume* of moral issues seem overwhelming to many people. At the same time, many parents have become alarmed because some young people seem to reject traditional values and appear unable to develop clearly thought-out, justifiable ethical principles.

Many adults feel that the school should have a role in the moral instruction of children. In the Seventh Annual Gallup Poll on Education, which was reported in December of 1975, 79% of those questioned favored "instruction in the schools that would deal with morals and moral behavior." Only 15% of those polled were opposed to this kind of instruction. The Eighth Annual Gallup Poll on Education reported similar responses to a question about the responsibility of students in educating students for moral behavior. It seems clear that most adults feel that the schools should have a role in the moral education of students.

However, this does not answer the question of what kind of moral education. The apparent agreement of individuals on the need for instruction in moral behavior disappears when they must specify what will be done in the school. Should it be a good, old-fashioned type of lecturing or sermonizing to students about the virtues of hard work, honesty, loyalty, etc.? Should it be a program of corporal punishment for students who violate school rules? Should moral instruction concentrate on values clarification? Should it be a cognitive-developmental approach? Are students to develop their own thinking abilities, or are they to adopt the parents' or teachers' points of view? What topics or issues should be dealt with? These are just a few of the questions which arise when the time comes to implement an actual program in moral instruction.

Despite an apparent mandate from the people for such instruction, individuals who attempt to establish a moral education program in a school system must tread *carefully*. Values and moral education can be very sensitive topics despite the fact that schools have always influenced students' moral development. An interesting assumption made by many people is that moral education has not been occurring in the school. This disregards the plethora of moral issues which are present in both the formal curriculum of the school and in the "hidden curriculum." This hidden curriculum includes the lessons that schools teach as a result of their organization, the way teachers, students and administrators interact with one another, etc. The assumption by some people that this is a new aspect of education, combined with the feeling that teachers may encroach upon parental rights, has made moral education a sensitive topic in some school districts.

Careful consideration must be given to the type of moral education program which will be implemented. What will its theoretical bases be? Will it be a subject added to what is already taught? Should it be at both the elementary and secondary levels? How will teacher education be accomplished? Will commercially prepared materials be used, or will "home-grown" materials be developed? How many teachers should be involved? How will they be selected? How much input should parents and community members have? These and many other questions must be answered either before or in the process of implementing such a program.

The Ethical Quest Project

The Ethical Quest in a Democratic Society in Tacoma, Washington, is an example of one attempt by a school district to respond to the challenge for more effective moral or ethical education. The Tacoma School District, with funding from the National Endowment for the Humanities, is conducting a program to stimulate the moral development of children at all grade levels. Looking at our experiences in establishing this program may provide some valuable insights about the compatability of formal programs in moral education with the public schools. Problems have been encountered and resolved which may well arise in other settings.

Our approach has been to create a program which encourages students to think in more complex and more just ways about moral issues in the curriculum and the classroom. We assume that young people must be able to recognize moral or ethical questions and know how to think in a rational way about the moral decisions to be made. They should learn how to take more people's points of view into consideration when making a decision. Our theoretical base has been cognitive-developmental. We try to stimulate students to move from limited, egocentric ways of thinking about moral issues to autonomous, principled ways.

Part of the importance of Tacoma's Ethical Quest Project is that it is in an urban school district with a sizeable percentage of working class families. There are 31,438 students in forty-three elementary schools, ten junior high schools, five senior high schools and one vocational-technical school. Tacoma has a population of 156,000 with many people working in the shipping, paper, smelting and manufacturing industries. Until now, most moral education programs have been conducted on a small scale in suburban schools. The perennial question has been, "You've done it in Newton or Brookline, Massachusetts, but can you do it in an urban school system?" The generalizability of moral education programs is enhanced by this project.

The number of teachers involved also makes this project unique. Most moral education programs have only involved a few teachers systematically. We currently have forty-five teachers involved from grades 1-12 and (by 1979) one hundred teachers will be participating. That will be the largest number of teachers involved in this type of program. In addition to those teachers directly involved, many others will be affected by the sharing of curriculum materials and readings, by discussions with project teachers and by in-service programs.

By the end of the project grant period, we plan to have a comprehensive in-service moral education program which can be used with any group of teachers. Readings, videotapes, discussions, etc., will be carefully structured to encourage teachers to become aware of the moral issues in the curriculum which they already teach, and to give them a theoretical framework for understanding moral education. They will also learn to create new materials and to use appropriate instructional strategies to stimulate the moral development of students, as well as becoming more aware of the moral issues which arise from adult and student behavior in the school (i.e., the "hidden curriculum"). This in-service process will allow school districts to introduce large numbers of teachers to moral education in a systematic way.

A major problem which moral education must face, if it is to be a significant portion of the school curriculum, is *how* to give teachers the requisite knowledge and abilities. Much of moral education has been based upon the apprenticeship system — a master craftsman teaching a few students the skills of the trade. This model works well with small numbers of teachers, but if we want to expand our influence to the majority of teachers we must have systematic processes for educating them about moral development.

Building School and Community Support

Any school program, but especially one in moral education, needs support from within the school system and also from the community, since such programs are potentially controversial. Creating support and neutralizing opposition are essential for the success of a program in moral education. Our experience in Tacoma is instructive in this respect.

The people who were most opposed to the Ethical Quest Project generally felt that such a program would infringe on

Sullivan and Dockstader

their rights as parents and/or would be anti-religious. Part of the problem in describing the program and creating a base of support was that we did not have concrete examples of what would be happening in the classroom. We were only starting to examine the curriculum and develop materials. There were no ready-made curriculum packages to be examined.

Much time was spent in talking to groups in the community: parents, community leaders and interested citizens. We explained our aims and listened carefully to their feelings and concerns. Those individuals who had not already made up their minds were favorably impressed by a simple, straight-forward explanation of what the program was and was not. But it was important to really listen, and to respond to any concerns which individuals might express.

The director and coordinator began working on the project during February, 1976. February to June was spent working with twenty-three teachers in initial curriculum examination and planning for a curriculum development and teacher-training workshop in June. During this formative phase a small-but-vocal minority in the community raised objections to the program. Fortunately, we had developed a strong base of support among parents, educators and other community members.

We also prepared simple, concise written materials which described the program in jargon-free language. These materials were sent to anyone who requested information. They provided a good overview of our plans and, so, tended to calm any anxieties people might have. They were especially helpful in reaching people who could not attend meetings or come into our office to find out about the project.

As we began to evolve actual materials which would be used in the program, many of those who had been concerned initially or whose concern had been aroused by others were reassured. By the end of the June, 1976 workshop most objections to the project had disappeared. There was a small number of individuals who were still adamantly opposed to anything we might do, but we had a solid base of support from people in the community.

During the early stages of the project, we also formed a citizens' advisory committee to work with the project. We hoped the committee would reassure concerned citizens that responsible members of the community were reviewing our work. The members of the committee also were able to get information about the project out to various groups in the community. We involved people from many segments of the community on the advisory committee: business, labor, police, parents, universities, media, teachers, program opponents, religious groups, and professional people. Meetings of the advisory committee were open to the public. The committee reviewed project activities and curriculum development work, observed teaching activities, and participated in teacher workshops. This advisory committee reassured some of those who were fearful about the project during its early phases and contributed valuable suggestions to our program.

At the same time that we built community support for the project, we also worked to assure support from within the school system. Significant opposition from faculty, administrators or school board members could have delayed, altered or ended the program. We met with the principals of those schools where teachers were participating in the Ethical Quest Project to brief them on the objectives and progress of the program. Because the principals were informed, they were able to answer questions from parents. We also made presentations to faculty groups and distributed written materials to anyone who had questions. District administrators were also given reports on the program, and they provided another source of positive information for parents and community members. Since the superintendent was one of the original architects of the program, there has been strong support from the upper levels of administration downward.

The school board was also a key group to be kept informed. Those who opposed the Ethical Quest Project called and sent letters to the board members and requested an opportunity to speak at one of the regular board meetings.

Sullivan and Dockstader

Fortunately, we had given reports to the board, provided them with written materials, and had met with some of the board members individually. Board members had even been invited to participate in planning workshops for the project.

When the opponents of the program spoke at a school board meeting in May of 1976, the board was well-prepared to deal with their criticisms. A number of respected members of the community also spoke in favor of the program at that meeting. This provided strong reinforcement for the board members to stand firm. Community support helped to generate board support and vice versa.

Both community and school system support were essential to the success and, indeed, the survival of the Ethical Quest Project. All school programs, but especially one related to moral education, must carefully build both bases of support. Without such support they are vulnerable to pressures from the community.

CURRICULUM DEVELOPMENT

Importance

A major focus of the Ethical Quest Project is curriculum development. If we operate under the assumption that moral development is a priority, the school curriculum provides an opportunity to stimulate that development in students. It has been shown that moral reasoning can become more complex and more differentiated as a result of carefully structured educational experiences. Work of Mosher and Sprinthall at Harvard,[1] Sprinthall and his associates and students at Minnesota,[2] and Mosher and his students at Boston University[3] has demonstrated that students' moral development can be stimulated by courses in the schools.

Much of the early work in moral education involved separate, distinct courses. This had the advantage of allowing teachers to concentrate exclusively on stimulating students' moral development. The content of a course was selected for this specific purpose, rather than to teach history or literature. However, we felt it would be more advantageous to create a curriculum development process which can be applied to any subject area. Our purpose has not been to add an additional "subject" to elementary teachers' already saturated schedules, or another elective at the secondary level, but to integrate a concern for ethical issues into the humanities curricula.

Working with the existing curriculum also effectively counters the arguments that moral education will take time from the basic curriculum. We feel that moral education must become an integral part of the school curriculum, if it is to be an important force in education today. Therefore, we are focusing on the abundant moral issues which are already present in the English, the Social Studies and the Health courses—the heart of the humanities program in the Tacoma schools. We want to widen students' exposure to moral issues and encourage them to confront these issues in a variety of contexts. This approach stresses reasoning and decision-making processes. The purpose of developing these materials is to ensure that students gain the skills necessary for them to reason effectively about moral issues, to make fair and just decisions in conflict situations, and to provide the stimulation necessary for students' moral development.

Process

Initial curriculum development and teacher education involved a core group of twenty-three teachers from nine elementary, junior high and senior high schools. These teachers were chosen from among a large number of volunteers representing nearly every school in the district. We selected skilled teachers from those schools where there was a concentration of interest in moral education. Hunt and Metcalf have shown that being a skilled teacher is a necessary prerequisite to becoming an effective moral educator.[4] We have found that the most effective teachers in this project are those who are able to listen to the reasoning presented by students about a moral issue, to question the students' thinking, and to facilitate interaction among the students. Participation by more than one teacher at a particular school is also important, because it enables teachers to work together and provides a source of mutual support. This mutual support was essential during the initial phases of the Ethical Quest Project, when a small but vociferous group in the community expressed skepticism and even opposition.

The core teachers participated in a two-week training workshop in November, 1975; scholars in the field of moral education provided an intensive orientation, based on recent developments in moral theory and instruction. From January to June of 1976, the core teachers continued to familiarize themselves with theories of ethical development and to explore the educational implications of those theories. Concurrently, they met in small groups to examine specific curriculum areas. The working groups were formed according to grade level and subject matter (English, Social Studies or Health). Each of these groups began by looking carefully at what is known about the developmental level of the students (e.g., their cognitive, ego, emotional, social and moral levels). They then spent a substantial amount of time analyzing the materials that they had been teaching. They identified the moral issues which were present in their curricula and began to design supplemental materials and teaching strategies appropriate to the developmental level of their students which highlight these issues. It is impossible to deal effectively with a topic like the American Revolution without considering the ethical decisions which the colonists faced (e.g., Was the overthrow of an established political system justified?). Likewise, ethical conflicts are an integral and essential element in understanding literary works from Shakespeare to Steinbeck.

A substantial amount of work was done during in-service days in the Spring of 1976, and during a three-week workshop held in June. James Shaver from Utah State University, and Ralph Mosher and Paul Nash from Boston University were among the consultants present with expertise in the field of moral education to work with the teachers. The resulting course materials were used during the 1976-77 school year. Changes were made during that year on the basis of the teachers' experience with the materials. Supervision of teachers by project staff and evaluation of curriculum materials were also ongoing processes during the 1976-77 school year.

During the Spring of 1977, twenty-two additional teachers were added to the core group. A three-day orientation was held in May to acquaint these new people with the basic approaches to ethical development and with what had been done by the original core group of teachers. The new educators also began to identify the courses and ethical issues on which they planned to focus.

An intensive, three-week workshop for all forty-five teachers was held in June of 1977 that was similar to the session conducted the preceding year for the core group of twenty-three. New teachers had an opportunity during this three-week period to assimilate ethical development theory, and to design materials for classroom use. The original core group of teachers spent part of the time revising what they had taught during the preceding year. Their remaining time was devoted to designing new materials and teaching strategies, or to functioning as consultants for the new teachers. Again, experts in the field of ethics and moral education were present, as resources, during much of the workshop period.

All forty-five teachers in the Ethical Quest Project are currently using the materials developed with students from grades 1-12. The project staff has been supervising teachers and assisting with the implementation of these new materials. A careful evaluation will be made of the curriculum, and we shall attempt to measure the effects on students. This is a continuing cycle of clinical research and development.[5]

146   Sullivan and Dockstader

Materials

This section will attempt to relate the approach we have described to some actual curriculum examples which have been developed by the Ethical Quest Project. In order to do that, we shall analyze some specific lessons at the elementary, junior high and senior high levels.

A. An Elementary School Unit on Rules

The elementary school teachers worked first on a combined social studies and language arts unit on rules. The materials are designed for the upper elementary level, but can be adapted for use with grades three through six. The teachers felt that elementary students needed to know not only that rules exist but, also, why we have them, how they are made and how they can be changed. Many of the moral issues which elementary students face are concerned with rules.

The unit begins with sections on those rules which are closest to the child's experience (i.e., home rules and school rules); these are followed by sections on rules and laws in the community and the nation. We try to move the students gradually outward from their immediate experience with rules to more distant, abstract levels. A variety of instructional strategies are used in the unit, including group and individual reading, class discussions, role-plays, writing assignments, interviews of adults and other students, debates, and class meetings. Lessons are designed to be used with groups of students of wide-ranging academic abilities. We have provided the detail of one of these lessons in *Table I.*

The lesson in *Table I* attempts to have students understand why we have rules from the perspectives of other people. Often rules seem arbitrary and without reason to students. Understanding the reasons for rules, and that other people in the school may see the rules differently, is a major step in learning the principles of social organ-

---
TABLE I   SAMPLE LESSON FOR ELEMENTARY SCHOOL STUDENTS:
               UNIT ON RULES (Ethical Quest Project).

TOPIC or THEME: "I WONDER WHY"

Below is a list of fifteen school rules. Following each rule are some unfinished
sentences. You are to think about w h y each rule was made and finish each
sentence with a reason why the person named might think that rule was made.

Example: Why was this rule made? A student may check out two library books.

    +   A librarian might say . . . "Many students use our library, and I want all
                                     to be able to find books."

    +   A principal might say . . . "Our school budget limits the number of books
                                     we buy. Therefore, we have to limit the
                                     number of books a student checks out.

Complete the following sentences, telling w h y each rule was made. Try to put
yourself in the role of the person that is mentioned. Write what you think that
person would say.

   1. Rule: There is to be no running in the building at any time, except in
             organized games in the gym.

      a. A principal might say . . .

      b. A teacher might say . . .

      c. A parent might say . . .

   2. Rule: No one is to leave the school grounds after they arrive any time
             during the day, without permission of a teacher or the principal,
             except when going home for lunch.

      a. A parent might say . . .

      b. A principal might say . . .

   3. Rule: No rock-throwing at any time.

      a. A playground supervisor might say . . .

      b. A principal might say . . .

      c. Another student might say . . .

      d. A parent might say . . .

   4. Rule: No fighting at any time.

      a. A principal might say . . .

      b. A parent might say . . .

      c. Another student might say . . .
---

ization. By role-playing the children are encouraged to look
at the situation from the points of view of several people, not
just from their own immediate perspective. The ability to
take the role of others (i.e., to understand that other people
have feelings, ideas, points of view different from oneself)
and to see oneself from others' points of view is an essential
element in the intellectual and moral development of students.

B. A *Junior High School Unit on Moral Reasoning*

We have also developed a junior high language arts curriculum which attempts to stimulate students' role-taking capacities and moral reasoning through literature and films. The various lessons encourage students to become aware of themselves and other people as individuals with differing thoughts, emotions, roles and points of view—a significant accomplishment in social role-taking. This is an especially important element in moving from preconventional to conventional moral reasoning, a transition which usually occurs in the junior high school years. Discussion of the moral issues in the films and literature is also emphasized.

TABLE II   SAMPLE LESSON FOR JUNIOR HIGH SCHOOL STUDENTS:
                UNIT ON MORAL REASONING (Ethical Quest Project).

TOPIC or THEME: "THE PEARL," by John Steinbeck

Activity: Discuss controversial aspects or hold debates on the following issues in The Pearl.

Purpose: To give students a chance to consider both sides of a problem, weigh the merits of each side and form their own opinions; to encourage them to listen closely to each other and paraphrase each other's ideas to be sure of understanding.

Preliminaries:
(1) Students read and discuss The Pearl.
(2) They discuss what happens and how.
(3) They have worked together to prepare a list of the events of the plot, as these occur over a 4-day period.

Process: If discussion, have students move desks into an oval, so each can see the others. Introduce a topic, draw conflicting ideas about it, probe w h y these ideas are held.

If debate:
(1) Divide class into groups of four students each;
(2) Let each group "draw" its own topic from a hat;
(3) Each group divides into two pro and two con speakers;
(4) Group has a known period of time to prepare arguments (e.g., 20 minutes);
(5) All groups present their ideas - - 1st pro speaker presents basic and best pro ideas; 1st con speaker presents basic and best con ideas; 2nd pro speaker tries to argue against the main objections presented by the con side; 2nd con speaker tries to argue against the main objections presented by the pro side;
(6) After a group has completed all four presentations, the rest of the class acts as a jury and decides which side presented the more convincing arguments.

Issues for Discussion and Debate: The Pearl.

A. The Issue of KILLING.

1. Is Kino justified in killing the four people he does?
2. What would you have done if you were Kino? Why?
3. Is killing someone ever justified? If so, when? If not, why not?
4. If Kino were brought to trial and you were on the jury, would you find him guilty of murder? Why, or why not?

```
------------------------------------------------------------------------
```
TABLE II   SAMPLE LESSON FOR JUNIOR HIGH SCHOOL STUDENTS:
(Cont'd)   UNIT ON MORAL REASONING (Ethical Quest Project).
```
------------------------------------------------------------------------
```

Issues for Discussion and Debate: The Pearl

A. The Issue of KILLING

    1. Is Kino justified in killing the four people he does?

    2. What would you have done if you were Kino? Why?

    3. Is killing someone ever justified? If so, when? If not, why not?

    4. If Kino were brought to trial and you were on the jury, would you find him guilty of murder? Why, or why not?

    5. Should Kino be punished by some kind of court sentence? What kind?

    6. What would be the best reason for a judge to give Kino some punishment?

    7. What would be the best reason for the judge not to punish him?

    8. Were there things he could have done to avoid these killings?

    9. If someone killed your best friend in self-devense, what would your reaction be? If someone killed a person you dislike a lot, how would you feel? Why? Is there any difference between these two? Should there be?

B. The Issue of CHEATING

    1. How do the pearl buyers cheat Kino?

    2. Do they have the right to offer him less than his pearl is worth? If yes, should they act on this right?

    3. If someone you knew had a bike which was worth $100.00, but he had to sell it right away because he needed money for his family, would it be right for you to try to buy it for $5.00? What if this person were a friend of yours?

    4. Do you think pearl buyers in the capitol would have been more honest with Kino, if he could have gotten there? Why, or why not?

    5. Is cheating ever justified? When? If not, why not?

    6. Why do people cheat?

C. The Issue of BEATING PEOPLE

    1. Why does Kino beat Juana?

    2. Is he justified in doing this? Should he have beat her?

    3. What would you have done, if you were in Kino's position?

    4. What else could he have done?

    5. Is beating someone up ever justified? If so, when? If not, why not?

    6. If you were Juana, would you have thought the beating was justified? Why?

D. The Issue of REFUSING HELP TO SOMEONE IN NEED

    1. Why does the doctor refuse to help Coyotito?

    2. Does a doctor have the right to refuse help to someone who needs help?

    3. Does he if the person might die without his help?

    4. What if a doctor was forced to help so many people who couldn't pay that the doctor became poor? (e.g., Need for Medicare, Medicaid programs.)

    5. Has anyone in real need ever asked you for help? What kind? What was your response? How did you feel?

    6. Should you ever risk your own life to help someone else? Would you?

```
------------------------------------------------------------------------
```

The Pearl is a short novel by John Steinbeck, appropriate for use at the junior high level. The lesson outlined in *Table II* engages students in discussions and debates of some of the novel's controversial moral issues. Such discussion is a fundamental way to stimulate moral development. Students learn the basics of debating ethical issues, including how to weigh the arguments on both sides of a moral issue, how to listen carefully to what other people say, and how to come to a reasonable and reasoned position. When exploring these issues, they come to terms with how they feel about cheating or stealing (for instance), as well as what The Pearl says about them. The novel serves as a stimulus for the students to examine their own moral principles and judgments.

C. A High School Unit on Moral Action

The high school unit outlined in *Table III* presents the students with the basic dilemma/conflict of the Caine Mutiny Court Martial, even before they read it or see the movie. Students confront the situation faced by Lieutenant Maryk when he must decide whether or not to take command of the "Caine." They are asked to systematically examine each alternative and its moral implications, including the consequences which flow from each such alternative. Larger conceptual questions about justice, responsibility, duty, and respect for human life are also posed to the students. Students are asked to say not only what Maryk should do but, also, what *they* would and *should* do if they were in that situation. Any discrepencies which may exist between what they believe they would do and what they think they should do can then be examined. Students are also asked to put themselves in the place of members of the court martial board.

TABLE III   SAMPLE LESSON FOR SENIOR HIGH SCHOOL STUDENTS:
UNIT ON MORAL ACTION (Ethical Quest Project).

TOPIC or THEME: "CAINE MUTINY COURT MARTIAL"

Dilemma
Objective: Explore the conflicts of duty, rules and concern for human life.

Mutiny
Dilemma: Lieutenant Maryk is the executive officer aboard the "USS Caine"'"
during World War II. Maryk is conscientious, loyal and very
capable. He is also very concerned about the ship's captain.
He feels Captain Queeg has consistently shown paranoid behavior
in the unjust and irrational treatment of the men, and the bizarre
running of the ship. Yet the "Caine" has never been in an endan-
gered position before. Lieutenant Keefer, a writer, and the
other ship's officers are also acutely aware of Captain Queeg's
psychological problem. In fact, Maryk and Keefer at one time
had almost reported the situation to the admiral of the fleet, but
backed out because of the consequences, and lack of support
from keefer.

The "Caine" gets caught in a severe typhoon, in which Captain
Queeg's irrational judgment is threatening the ship's safety.
Lieutenant Maryk is torn between his sense of loyalty and duty
and his realization that Queeg's behavior and poor judgment
may sink the ship with the loss of many lives.

Discussion
Questions: a. What are Maryk's alternatives?

        b. What are the consequences of each alternative?

        c. Is there any way that Maryk and the other officers could
help Queeg?

        d. What is an act of mutiny?

        e. What is the punishment for mutiny?

        f. What would you do if you were Maryk?

        g. Is what Maryk thinking of doing really mutiny?

        h. Why is the punishment for mutiny so severe?

        i. What is loyalty? Duty? Responsibility?
Is there any conflict among these three?

        j. What is justice? Fairness?

        k. Is justice and fairness the same for each person or situation?

        l. If Maryk took command of the "Caine," and later was brought
before a court martial board on which you had the deciding
vote, would you vote to convict or acquit him? Why? Is it
ever right to break the law? Why, or why not?

        m. If Maryk were found guilty, what punishment would you
give to him? Why?

        n. What is the purpose of punishing someone who breaks
the law?

Read
and View: The Caine Mutiny Court Martial.

Follow-up
Discussion: (e.g., reconsider earlier answers to Discussion Questions.)

Writing
Instruction and
Assignment: Discuss the concept of justice and fairness in terms of
Queeg, Maryk and Keefer.

               Is justice and fairness the same for all three, or is it
different for each one?

               Be specific with support from the play, and any other sources
familiar to you.

Teacher Education

An essential element of any moral education program is teacher education. In the Ethical Quest Project, teacher education has been closely tied to the curriculum development process. One of our major goals is for teachers to become capable of analyzing the curricula which they teach, to identify the moral issues in those curricula, and to develop teaching strategies around the issues so identified. It is very difficult to separate these processes.

A first step in the process of teacher education was for teachers to become *aware* of what a moral issue is and what psychology and philosophy say about moral development. Teachers read primary and secondary source materials about a range of philosophical and psychological theories relating to moral development. These theories and their implications for teaching were discussed. Videotapes of classroom applications of the theories were presented. Teachers examined and questioned the basic assumptions underlying various theories. Teachers should understand how an individual's moral reasoning develops from childhood to adulthood.

We also tried to improve teachers' *skills* in several ways. Their ability to lead discussions and ask questions is essential. We stressed the importance of asking *why* when students make statements about moral issues (i.e., of asking for the reasons behind a statement). Teachers also learned how to use other types of questions in order to facilitate discussion and focus students' attention on the central moral issues, or to encourage student-to-student interaction. The ability to ask various types of questions is a basic skill for teachers involved in moral education. Videotapes of class discussions were used to illustrate the process of conducting moral discussions generally, and of asking questions specifically.

The teachers learned to use various types of *instructional strategies* to focus on moral issues, and to stimulate students' thinking and development. Some of these strategies include: role-playing, discussions, debates, interviewing, class meetings, films, individual and small group work, journals, and writing assignments. Using different strategies to approach moral issues gives the student a rich and varied experience. They are less likely to get bored than if only one instructional technique is used. We provided examples of how these techniques have been used in various curricula, and we have worked with the teachers in applying these strategies to their own classrooms.

After the initial phase of teacher education, when teachers became familiar with theories of moral development and improved their instructional competencies, the teachers applied this new knowledge to the curricula they taught. We also encouraged teachers to be ready to deal with the moral issues which arise day-to-day in the classroom. These issues may develop from interactions among students and teachers in the classroom, from occurrences around the school or in the community, and from stories in the newspaper. It is important for the teacher to be ready to deal with those immediate issues which develop naturally in the course of the school experience.

When teachers began working with groups of students around the moral issues in the curriculum, we tried to provide supervisory help. We observed classes, and we tried to provide constructive feedback to the teachers. This is extremely important. It is one thing to read about theories, to develop one's questioning skills and, even, to write curriculum; it is more difficult to apply new skills in the classroom. Our observations pointed out to teachers areas on which they needed to work. As part of this supervision process we also have co-taught classes with teachers in the project. They then got a chance to see certain teaching skills modeled and, also, to realize that even those experienced in moral education do not have perfect classes.

Conclusion

Moral education can go on in an urban public school environment despite the crisis of confidence which the schools are experiencing. It is *not* inevitable that there will be a collision between values education and American schools. Moral education has always gone on in the schools. The content of the curriculum and the interaction of people in the school building make this unavoidable. The question is how effectively and how ethically moral education programs can be implemented.

Is it better for schools and teachers to avoid the important moral questions or to deal with them haphazardly, than it is to acknowledge those questions as a central part of the educational experience? Certainly there is a danger that teachers (or schools) will simply indoctrinate students with specific sets of beliefs. But it is naive to assume that this will not occur if we do not have programs which focus teacher attention on these issues. In fact, we believe that the danger of indoctrination is substantially greater if teachers and administrators do not learn how to deal effectively, and justly, with moral issues.

However, after establishing the need for effective curriculum development and teacher education, we still must decide how to proceed. Our experience with the Ethical Quest Project in Tacoma suggests *one possible approach* and has produced some *valuable guidelines*, which other school districts may wish to use in order to minimize the risk of a "collision." Careful thought and planning are necessary prerequisites before embarking on a program of moral education. This may not eliminate problems, but it should help to minimize them.

REFERENCES

1. Mosher, R. L. and N. A. Sprinthall, et. al.,"Psychological Education:
A Means to Promote Personal Development During Adolescence,"
in *The Counseling Psychologist*, 1971, 1 (4), 3-82.

Atkins, V. S. *High School Students Who Teach: An Approach to
Personal Learning.* (Unpublished doctoral dissertation, Graduate
School of Education, Harvard University, 1972).

Dowell, R. C. *Adolescents as Peer Counselors: A Program for Psychological Growth.* (Unpublished doctoral dissertation, Graduate
School of Education, Harvard University, 1971).

Greenspan, B. *Facilitating Psychological Growth in Adolescents
through Child Development Curricula.* (Unpublished doctoral
dissertation, Graduate School of Education, Harvard University,
1974).

2. Erickson, V. L. *Psychological Growth for Women: A Cognitive-
Developmental Curriculum Intervention.* (Unpublished doctoral
dissertation, University of Minnesota, 1973).

Rustad, K. *Teaching Counseling Skills to Adolescents: A Cognitive-
Developmental Approach to Psychological Education.* (Unpublished doctoral dissertation, University of Minnesota, 1974).

3. Grimes, P. M. *Teaching Moral Reasoning to Eleven-Year-Olds and
Their Mothers: A Means of Promoting Moral Development.* (Un-
published doctoral dissertation, School of Education, Boston
Universtiy, 1974).

Paolitto, D. P. *Role-taking Opportunities for Early Adolescents:
A Program in Moral Education* (Unpublished doctoral dissertation,
School of Education, Boston University, 1975).

Sullivan, P. J. *A Curriculum for Stimulating Moral Reasoning and
Ego Development in Adolescents.* (Unpublished doctoral dissertation, School of Education, Boston University, 1975).

4. Hunt, M. P. and L. E. Metcalf. *Teaching High School Social Studies.*
(New York: Harper and Row, 1968).

5. Mosher, R. L. "Knowledge from Practice: Clinical Research and
Development in Education," in *The Counseling Psychologist*, 1974,
4 (4), 73-82.

Mosher, R. L. "Funny Things Happen on the Way to Curriculum
Development," in H. J. Peters and R. F. Aubrey (Eds.), *Guidance:
Strategies and Techniques.* (Denver: Love Publishing, 1975).